Excellent
IT Leadership

DAVID E McKEAN

About the Author and IT Leaders

DAVID MCKEAN IS A FORMER CIO WHO HAS WORKED FOR SEVERAL MULTINATIONAL COMPANIES AROUND THE WORLD. THROUGH HIS work with over one thousand course delegates and interviews with some of the top IT managers and CIOs worldwide, he knows what it takes to succeed as an IT professional.

Building on the first book in the series, *Excellent IT Management,* *Excellent IT Leadership* looks at the five most important behaviors of successful IT leaders: personal leadership, leading IT teams, influencing people/building networks, technology innovation, and corporate leadership.

The books are the basis for the training courses Excellent *IT Management* and *Excellent IT Leadership*, run globally through a network of partners. They are run as both public and in-house courses and as interactive, live online programs. They are based on the experiences of our delegates and additional interviewees with leading CIOs.

If you have any comments or management learning that you would like to be considered for future editions, please feel free to e-mail David at david.mckean@itleaders.co.uk.

David McKean
IT Leaders, Greenlands, Henley-on-Thames, Oxfordshire, RG9 3AU, UK
E-mail: david.mckean@itleaders.co.uk
Telephone: (+44) 1491-57-86-88 (UK) or (+1) 203-810-6143 (US)

Contents

1.   **Personal Coach**...1
1.1   Emotional Intelligence..1
1.2   IT Management Styles..4
1.3   Successful CIO Behaviors.......................................6
1.4   Where Successful IT Managers Spend Time 9
     1.4.1   Busy Fools..9
     1.4.2   Urgent or Important?.........................10
1.5   Change Your Time Profile 14
1.6   Create Your Own Brand...16
     1.6.1   Product Packaging 16
     1.6.2   Branded by Our Actions....................18
     1.6.3   Quality of the Goods and Service......19
     1.6.4   An exercise in Building Our Own Brand 19
1.7   Make Your Changes Count....................................24

Collect Your Thoughts...26

2.   **Team Leadership** 27
2.1   Recruit Good People...28
3.1   IT Organization..30
     3.1.1   Organizational Structures..................30
     3.1.2   Clear Roles and Responsibilities........31
2.2   Create Harmony 32
2.3   Creating a Balance of Skills 36
2.4   Set Direction and Objectives 39
2.5   Create a Good Working Environment 41

2.6 Develop Skills..42
    2.6.1 Delegate and Coach...42
    2.6.2 Team Meetings 44
    2.6.3 Business Meetings..44
    2.6.4 Training Courses 45
    2.6.5 Use Vendors and Networks.................................46
    2.6.6 Networking...46
2.7 Manage Performance 46
2.8 Rewards and Recognition 48

3. **Effective Networking**...**51**
3.1 Relationship Campaigns..51
3.2 Rapport and Credibility 55
3.3 The Client's Viewpoint...56
3.4 Influencing Outcomes...63
3.5 Guiding Conversations..67
3.6 High-Level Influence...70
3.7 Politics and the Balance of Power.....................................73

4. **Technology Innovation** **79**
4.1 The Innovation Role of the CIO 79
4.2 A Culture of Innovation 81
4.3 The Process of Innovation...84
4.4 Finding Problems to Innovate 87
4.5 Techniques for Generating Ideas 91
4.6 From Ideas to Implementation 95
4.7 Measuring IT Innovation...98
4.8 Lanterns to the Future 100
4.9 Some Examples of Innovation 102

5. **Corporate Leadership** **107**
5.1 The New Role of the CIO 107
5.2 A Player not a Spectator 109
5.3 Align IT Results to the Business...111
5.4 A Model for IT to Business Alignment................................113
5.5 Create a Strategy for IT Alignment....................................114

5.6   Align Results—IT Governance.. 115
       5.6.1   Project performance.. 117
       5.6.2   Performance Against Targets.................................... 118
       5.6.3   Risk and Compliance.. 120
       5.6.4   IT Governance Structures.. 123
5.7   Ten Examples of Governance 124
       5.7.1   A Small or Medium Enterprise (SME)...................... 127
       5.7.2   A Research Company.. 128
       5.7.3   A Manufacturing Company...................................... 129
       5.7.4   A Company with Outsourced IT............................... 131
       5.7.5   An International Law Firm.. 132
       5.7.6   Financial Services 133
       5.7.7   A Telecoms Turnaround... 134
       5.7.8   A Government Department....................................... 135
       5.7.9   A Logistics Company... 136
       5.7.10   A Charity 137
5.8   Align People to Enhance Perception..................................... 138

6.   Secrets of Success.. 143
6.1   The IT Leaders Top Ten List.. 143
6.2   Ingredients of World-class IT... 146
6.3   Excellent IT Management—Leadership Opportunities........... 151
       6.3.1   IT Strategist... 152
       6.3.2   Project and Business Change Leader 153
       6.3.3   Performance Pioneer... 154
       6.3.4   Crisis Commander.. 155
       6.3.5   Commercial Expert... 156
6.4   Excellent IT Leadership—Leadership Opportunities 157
       6.4.1   Personal Coach 157
       6.4.2   Technology Innovator 159
       6.4.3   Team Captain... 161
       6.4.4   Executive connector.. 162
       6.4.5   Business Champion 164
6.5   The First Ninety Days.. 167
       6.5.1   Why Is This a Critical Time? 168
       6.5.2   Before You Start... 169

6.5.3		Weeks One and Two	170
6.5.4		Weeks Three and Four	171
6.5.5		Weeks Five and Six	174
6.5.6		Weeks Seven and Eight	176
6.5.7		Weeks Nine to Twelve	176

7.   **In Conclusion** **179**
7.1   Take Time to Reflect 179
7.2   Next Steps 179
7.3   And Finally.. 179

8. Bibliography.. **181**

9. About the Author **187**

The Secret to Good IT Leadership

THIS BOOK IS BASED ON THE EXPERIENCES OF OVER ONE THOUSAND SENIOR IT MANAGERS AND CIOS AND PRESENTS THEIR GUIDELINES FOR success. It contains my own experiences in the singular and also those of my company IT Leaders, course delegates, and the various senior IT professionals we have worked with, in the plural. This book presumes you are an experienced IT manager and are looking for new ideas to improve your IT organization and boost your career success.

Excellent IT Leadership will give you the inside track on successful IT leadership. We reveal the secrets for success, together with some tools and techniques to aid you, all within a coherent framework that has been five years in the making. The aim is to help you maximize your skills, so you can fulfill your true potential.

The development of IT leadership skills presents a constant dilemma. Most IT managers are promoted from a technical position that relies on technical skills, and yet these skills count for very little in their new IT management post. Many managers respond by "keeping their hand in"—in other words, interfering. They get frustrated because they perceive themselves to be less valuable than they were before. As one manager told us, "It feels like being chosen for the tennis team because I was once good at swimming."

BEN'S STORY: WHAT NOW, BOSS?

I remember vividly my first job as an IT director. I was working for a large organization in Cape Town, South Africa. I had arrived at my hotel at 2:00 a.m. after a long flight. My management team, seeking to impress me with their enthusiasm, had arranged to meet me at 8:00 a.m. that morning. I looked at them through bloodshot eyes as they asked eagerly, "What should we do now, Boss?" It was a seminal moment for me. The plain truth was that I had no idea. The people around the table knew a lot more than I did. As I found out later, new managers often have this feeling of being out of their depth, of feeling like a bit of a fraud. Apparently, it is known as "Imposter syndrome." In truth, no new manager can ever possibly know everything from the outset. Fortunately, in my case, I stumbled through by asking a number of smart questions, and I used the experience of the team to guide me.

The plain truth is that IT management is very different from IT, and IT leadership is very different from IT management. To be successful, one needs a regular review of what you are doing and frequent realignment to changing business priorities. This is different from most day-to-day IT roles, where the work is fairly well-defined. Our analysis of IT managers shows that success is about fulfilling a number of important roles in ever changing proportions. There are ten roles in total—five are described in our first book, *Excellent IT Management*, and five as part of this one, *Excellent IT Leadership*.

The roles are as follows:

Excellent IT Management

1. IT Strategist—putting together effective IT plans and strategies

2. Business Change Leader—working with business sponsors to deliver successful projects and business change

3. Performance Pioneer—creating and delivering a culture of continual service improvement

4. Crisis Commander—being prepared for the worst and leading from the front

5. Commercial Expert—IT financial management, sourcing strategy, negotiating good IT contracts, and working successfully with IT partners

Excellent IT Leadership

1. Personal Coach—making the most of your time, building your personal brand, and taking control of your career

2. Team Captain—creating a culture of success and leading technology teams

3. Executive Connector—networking effectively and influencing other senior managers

4. Technology Innovator—identifying new technologies, creating an innovation culture, and generating new ideas

5. Business Champion—working with the board to lead the business forward

All the CIOs we interviewed for this book are avid readers. Throughout the footnotes of this book, you will find references to some excellent books that have been a source of inspiration to many.

This book is a practical guide for experienced managers, and as such, you will certainly find some ideas familiar. I hope that you will bear with me during these parts; I am confident that elsewhere you will find a host of new ideas that will benefit you and your organization.

1. Personal Coach

FEW IT MANAGERS ARE FORTUNATE ENOUGH TO HAVE THEIR OWN BUSINESS COACH OR MENTOR. THOSE WHO DO WILL HAVE NOTICED some changes in approach over the last few years. The modern business coach works with the coachee[1] and helps them work through problems for themselves. And since most IT managers do not have a coach, this is a skill that they need to develop. In other words, our first role as a successful IT manager is to act as our own personal business coach. This means understanding strengths and weaknesses, working through problems in a structured way, making good (career) decisions, and last but no means least, taking control of our career success.

1.1 EMOTIONAL INTELLIGENCE

So, what are the skills that we need to develop to be successful? Companies have been preoccupied for years with this question, trying to understand the most important leadership traits that deliver the best business results. In the 1990s, Daniel Goleman[2] wrote a brilliant and highly recommended paper called "What Makes a Leader?" He worked with many organizations to find out which managers were considered their best leaders. His work was based on the business results of those managers and the opinions of their peers. The research identified five key skills, namely self-awareness, self-regulation, motivation, empathy, and social skill, which collectively, he called "emotional intelligence."

---

1 A rather ugly word to mean the person they are coaching.

2 Daniel Goleman, "What Makes a Leader?" *Harvard Business Review* (1998).

This list really resonates with many IT managers. When IT managers are asked to identify what distinguished the best bosses they have ever worked for, the answers include being a good listener, having a good sense of humor (actually the most common response), being trustworthy, being knowledgeable, and so on. All of these are directly attributable to emotional intelligence.

Three of the five characteristics—self-awareness, self-regulation, and motivation—are to do with what we call personal leadership; in other words, the ability to manage yourself and fulfill your potential.

Recognizing one's strengths and weaknesses (self-awareness) is vital. Managers who are self-aware know where they are going. They set targets for themselves that are difficult and challenging but achievable. This track record of achievement gives them a self-confidence that rubs off on others. These managers are usually very honest people, guided by a set of personal principles. If you interview someone with high self-awareness, they will be able to tell you what their shortcomings are and also have strategies in place to overcome them.

Self-awareness comes from noticing the effect that we have on the things around us. Usually, the signs are there if we look for them. Sometimes, they may need pointing out. If you look back on the best bosses you have ever worked for, you will probably see that they were the ones who honestly told you what you were good at and what you needed to work on.

DAVID'S STORY: IN A GOOD MOOD

As it happened, shortly after I read the paper on emotional intelligence, I was given a stark reminder of the importance of self-awareness. I was based in Shanghai, busily working at my desk, when I looked up to see a queue forming outside my door. There were about five of my managers and other team members waiting in line to see me. Thinking that something was up, I asked my assistant what had caused this sudden rush of interest. She eventually admitted that she had sent a note out to the department, saying that I was "in a good mood" and that if any of them needed a favor (such as signing expenses), now might be a good time. This certainly made me smile (I really *was* in a good mood!), but as I reflected, it occurred to me that my own impression of myself was not how others saw me. I had no idea that I had such "good days" and "bad days." My self-awareness needed some work.

A good way to understand strengths and weaknesses is to do a 360-degree survey. This is where your manager, your peers, your direct reports, and end users or customers are asked to comment on your strengths and weaknesses. There are several methods in place to assist with these surveys. As an example, we work with the Hay 360 emotional competency inventory (www.haygroup.com), which is based on Goleman's emotional intelligence model.

Another assessment that you can easily carry out is called *Strengths Finder 2.0*[3]. This book, by Tom Rath, contains a code and a link to do the test online. It will identify your top five strengths. This reflects a changing attitude about leadership thinking. In the past, doing things better meant working on weaknesses. If we do have significant weaknesses (for example, poor delegation skills), then it is important to address them. In summary, though, it is more important to play to our strengths.

---

3 Tom Rath, *Strengths Finder 2.0*, (Washington, DC: Gallup Press, 2007).

1.2 IT MANAGEMENT STYLES

On our leadership course, we ask delegates to complete a psychometric questionnaire to help them understand what sort of manager they are. The assessment looks at their style of communication and can be life-changing for some managers. They come to realize that different managers behave in completely different ways, even when presented with the exact same situation. Every manager has a natural, preferred style of communicating that is a fundamental part of their character. As managers progress in their careers, they become more versatile in adapting to different methods, but fundamentally, their natural, preferred style never changes.

Think about which one describes you best. The four styles of communication are:

Logical and Structured: We have now assessed over one thousand IT managers. Not surprisingly, over 60 percent of IT managers fall into this category. These are people who like a lot of factual detail presented in a structured and logical way.	**High-Level Thinkers:** Studies suggest that approximately 70 percent of chief executives fall into this category and probably about 20 percent of IT managers. These people like information at a high level. They are easily bored and hate a lot of details.
Friendly: These are sociable people who live very much in the here and now. This type makes up 30 percent of the general population, but less than 5 percent of IT managers. They tend to be exceptional managers of people. They take care of people and have time to chat before getting down to business.	**Creative types:** Creative people think in terms of pictures and images. They are visionaries who see the future clearly. Often eloquent and artistic, they value relationships and can see possibilities for the future. About 15 percent of IT managers fall into this group.

TABLE 1. LEADERSHIP AND COMMUNICATION STYLES

Knowing our natural communication style is very important and determines how we relate to other managers. If you are not clear on which is your style, you could be facing the wrong way—in other words, communicating in the wrong style. We discuss this in more detail in Chapter 3.

Self-regulation is the other side of self-awareness. There is no point knowing what your weaknesses are if you don't do anything about them. Self-regulation is about regulating your emotions and keeping a balanced view of things. It means staying calm when someone comes to tell you that the payroll system has crashed or a key project needs to be delayed. Furthermore, self-regulated managers are more able to adjust to difficult situations. They are able to get to the heart of problems and ask relevant questions in a composed way. In contrast, managers who do not stay calm when presented with bad news will soon discover that people stop telling them what is going on.

Good self-regulation means putting strategies in place to overcome weaknesses. So, a manager who is (self) aware that they do not present well when rushed will always take the time to prepare properly. Self-regulation is that little voice inside you, talking through the different options and suggesting which one might work best in a particular situation.

The third personal characteristic of emotional intelligence is motivation. Managers with high motivation are always looking for ways to do things better. They never take "no" for an answer, although they usually won't take on the impossible. They like to keep score, so they can see positive progress.

JIM'S STORY: WHERE THERE'S A WILL

Jim was head of operations for a large organization in Indonesia. The company's main data center was out of date and needed replacing. Jim designed the layout and specified the equipment required. It turned out that all the equipment could be delivered within a few weeks, with the exception of the server racks. These would take several months and that assumed no problems with customs. Rather than delay the plan, he drafted a design with pencil and paper and set off to find a machine shop. After some searching, he found a company that was able to work to his drawings, and they handcrafted the racks in four weeks. A world-class data center was completed in just three months. Jim showed an extraordinary level of motivation. While others around him were already changing the completion date on the project plan, Jim was looking for a different way.

1.3 SUCCESSFUL CIO BEHAVIORS

Organizational hierarchies in today's world are much flatter than they used to be. This is a good thing, of course, but even within this new egalitarian society, managers are still expected to display different behaviors than their staff. In Table 2, you will find a list of what to do—and what *not* to do—to get ahead. The list was compiled by a leading headhunter, and it is based on her experience of working with top chief executives.

Impressing the CEO at the Interview	
Things to Do:	**Things Not to Do:**
1. Convey complex concepts in an interesting and clear way. Senior managers don't want drawn-out descriptions. They want to know what the technology can do for them.	1. Talk endlessly about technology.
	2. Be blissfully unaware of one's shortcomings. When asked about their weaknesses, poor candidates often say something like, "I suppose I sometimes work too hard," or "I don't suffer fools gladly." Better to have something a bit more interesting to say (although, stay away from admissions of embezzlement!)
2. Express yourself powerfully, and be able to answer questions thoughtfully and without too much detail, getting your point across clearly and persuasively.	
3. Demonstrate exceptional influencing skills, recognizing that different people are influenced by different things and influenced in different ways.	3. Go for any job. Managers should be discerning about which opportunities they apply for and should do their homework. Don't be one of those who turns up without knowing what the job is.
4. Be engaging and interesting with a sense of humor. Show an interest in new things and a thirst for knowledge.	4. Dress badly. IT executives should dress like their colleagues in other parts of the business. Ill-fitting suits, and hair that appears to have been cut with a knife and fork give a bad impression. Interestingly, in a straw poll of HR managers, over 50 percent said they pay attention to a candidate's shoes.
5. Be part of the inner sanctum: in every organization, there is a small group of five or six top managers who informally make all of the key decisions of the company. It includes the CEO, CFO, and generally two or three others. Not being aware of such a group is a sure sign that you are not part of it and not influencing things at the highest level.	5. Blame the business. The business "couldn't make up their minds," or "we had to educate the users in our new processes." Both of these patronizing phrases instantly suggest someone who does not respect or work closely with the user community.

TABLE 2. IMPRESSING THE CEO AT THE INTERVIEW

Let us focus on four behaviors in particular:

Dress Correctly: Whether you like it or not, first impressions basically come down to appearance—dress, haircut, shoes, accessories, and so on. Most people will tell you that their first impressions tend to be accurate. Even if they aren't, it can be quite some time before they change them. Without being prompted, it was interesting that over half the CIOs who we interviewed mentioned the importance of dressing correctly. All of them were wearing business suits or similar (both men and women), and more than half of the men were wearing ties.

A senior manager who is considering someone for a promotion will want proof that they can already do the job. The hiring manager will ask themselves, "Can I see this person in that job, in that chair?" Heavy metal T-shirts and nose piercings, for example, are just not helpful.

Communicate Well: Clear and concise language is vital, so no mumbling, rambling, losing the thread of conversation, or talking too much. Written communication should be clear and polite. One way to test this is to look at your e-mail "sent items." You will find the answer there. And what about spelling? Many top managers I've worked with were terrible spellers, but they always used spell check and asked people around them to quietly make any necessary corrections. Spelling may not be the same as management ability, but it still gives a bad impression.

Even the way a manager answers the phone is important. It is vital to return calls, get back to people, and deliver on commitments. Any single item weighed on its own may not be that important, but add them all together, and you have your behavior.

Make It Interesting: Having good conversational skills is very important. Being knowledgeable about your company or organization makes you interesting to your peers. Read the business press to find out what is happening in the marketplace, and look at your company's website on a regular basis to keep up to date on new product launches, financial results, and investor relations. And take time to understand new technology trends, so you can explain them clearly to others.

Be Streetwise: Many managers go about their business completely oblivious to the risks and consequences of what they are doing. We are not talking about financial risks. We are talking about career risks. These managers take on new projects without consideration as to what is needed and whether they have enough control to make things happen.

Compare that to the example of top athletes. Contrary to popular belief, they do not take on impossible challenges. They set difficult but achievable goals for themselves. When they master those goals, they look for the next ones. They follow a guided path in what is called the "Competition Zone" or the "C Zone."[4] They do not stay with one activity so long that it becomes boring—avoiding the so-called "drone zone." Equally, they avoid taking on challenges that are too difficult and lead them into the "panic zone." Over time, as their confidence and skills increase, they are able to take on greater and greater challenges. So, they are never out of control, and they never take something on without thinking.

1.4 WHERE SUCCESSFUL IT MANAGERS SPEND TIME

1.4.1 Busy Fools

When I ask managers how many e-mails they get a day, answers usually range from thirty to over one hundred. Those at the higher end are generally proud of this, and in some cases, e-mail completely defines their job and—to be honest—their lives. Unfortunately, these are often the very same managers who don't receive the recognition they deserve. For these managers, it is clear they need to work smarter and avoid being "busy fools."

---

4 Robert Kriegel and Marilyn Kriegel, *The Competition Zone: Peak Performance Under Pressure* (New York: Ballantine Books, 1994).

Ironically, time management is often one of the first management courses that managers attend. Guidelines generally say to stop procrastinating, handle things only once, group items together for when you call someone, and so on; in summary, how to get more done in a day. In among all these, there are two golden rules for IT managers:

- Have the right things on your list. As per the old adage, managers do things right, and leaders do the right things.

- Do them in order of priority, and put the big tasks into your calendar first. Think of your calendar as a fish tank with only so much space. Your large priority tasks are like rocks. You need to put these big rocks into your calendar first, and then spread the pebbles and sand (i.e., the smaller tasks) around them. This is the best way to make the most out of your available time.

1.4.2 Urgent or Important?

So, the first question is, "Which tasks should make it to the priority list?" To do this, we need to categorize our tasks. Every activity has two key characteristics. The first is its urgency—in other words, does it need to be done immediately, soon, or sometime in the future? The second is importance. Is it of high, medium, or low importance? Plotting these variables on a Boston matrix creates four possible combinations, which are labeled with a quadrant number in Figure 1. A task can therefore be:

- Quadrant 1—Urgent and important. This includes key reporting requirements, regular meetings, resolving immediate technical issues, crisis response, and so on.

- Quadrant 2—Important but not urgent. This includes longer-term activities, such as IT strategy, crisis planning, problem prevention, team building, and personal development.

- Quadrant 3—Urgent but not important. This includes less important meetings and lower priority e-mail and calls.

- Quadrant 4—Neither urgent nor important. This includes filing and administration activities, among other things.

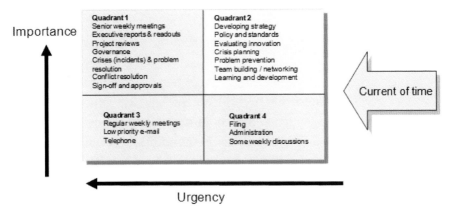

FIGURE 1. URGENT VS. IMPORTANT

How you categorize a task is entirely up to you. What is important to you may not be to someone else, although hopefully your boss would agree with your assessment.

All managers need to spend time in Quadrant 1 (urgent and impor-tant). It is just a question of how much. Although most managers think they should be spending more time in Quadrant 1 than any other, the research tells us otherwise[5]. **The most effective managers spend more time in Quadrant 2** (important but not yet urgent).

5 Steven R. Covey, *The 7 Habits of Highly Effective People*, (2004).

THE STORY OF LEO & MICHAEL

Our research has found that there are only small differences between successful and less successful managers. To illustrate this, we put together a DVD.[6] It tells a story of two IT managers who run similar organizations and have a similar day ahead of them. As we track their progress, we see that Leo (the leader) is well-prepared and working in Quadrant 2. Michael (the manager) is less prepared, spending a lot of time on detailed technical activities, always under time pressure, and much less effective. The punch line, though, is that both managers were played by television actor, David Gillespie. David could transform himself immediately from one character to another with a change of clothes and a change of what actors call "status," the characteristic that defines a person's confidence or lack of it. Actors are highly skilled at playing with status. The point is that many people who watch the video do not realize at first that it is the same person. Only small changes are needed to put across a completely different image.

What does this tell us? Simply put, the way to be effective is to address important tasks early before they become urgent. To take a technical example, a task that might be considered "important but not urgent" today—such as storage capacity planning—might suddenly translate into an urgent and important task when the disks are full. A neglected task that might have required half a day ahead of time, will then demand a week of several people's time.

There is effectively a current of time moving from the right to the left on Figure 1. So, if you sit on something that is not due until next week, it will drift from being not urgent today on the right-hand side of the matrix to becoming urgent on the left-hand side next week. Managers who do not recognize the

6 IT Leaders, *Leadership Time: The Story of Leo & Michael*, (Oxfordshire, United Kingdom: IT Leaders, 2009), DVD.

importance of doing things ahead of time find themselves constantly fighting fires. This increases stress levels and reduces performance. (Perhaps you know some managers who fall into this category.)

Activities in Quadrant 2 are often, but not always, leadership-type activities. They are typically larger in scope and usually involve other people, either team members or peers around the organization. They include business and IT strategy, high-level governance, problem prevention, and your own private goals.

Quadrant 2 tasks make the biggest difference to your performance and effectiveness.

Some managers will need to spend more time in quadrant 1 than others, due to the nature of their work. For example, incident desk managers will generally be involved with calls from users who have a problem right now, rather than sometime next week. These managers will still need to dedicate time to Quadrant 2 activities, such as root-cause analysis, to reduce the number of repeat calls. One organization we worked with found that over 15 percent of calls to the incident desk were for password resets. Some preplanning would have easily identified that the password format was too complicated and saved weeks of extra work.

Quadrant 3 tasks—the ones that are urgent but not important— often include routine weekly meetings, lower priority e-mails, and so on. "Not important" should really be called "less important," as it is unlikely that an activity is completely unnecessary. Think about how to achieve the same outcome in less time. For example, a weekly meeting might be very helpful, but if it could be done in thirty minutes rather than an hour, the time spent on a per-minute basis would make it twice as important.

Quadrant 4 activities are the "neither urgent nor important" tasks, such as the worst of e-mail. Examples might include weekly news bulletins that are full of advertisements masquerading as stories, spending too

much time smartening up a presentation, or creating a long report that no one reads. Don't confuse "not important" with "boring." Team members who don't complete their expenses on time, for example, should organize themselves better.

1.5 CHANGE YOUR TIME PROFILE

There is nothing more important (or obvious) to achieving career success than changing where your time is spent. Here are five steps to improving your time management.

1. **Write Down Your Business and Personal Objectives:** Some of these will come from your personal development plan, others you should add in yourself, particularly around career development. Use the form in Table 3 to list your thoughts.

2. **Look at Your Current Activities:** Work out how much time you spend on each one. Plot them on the urgent vs. important matrix, using a relative scale with respect to their objectives. There is no value putting everything in Quadrant 1 or Quadrant 2. Put "less important" tasks in Quadrant 3 or 4.

3. **Retain Key Activities:** Highlight activities that are a key part of your job and need to be retained; for example, the delivery of projects, operational management, budget management, and so on.

4. **Out with the Old:** If improving performance means changing what you do, you will need to free up some time before adding anything new. (Unless, of course, you are not very busy at the moment). Look through your calendar and e-mail, and put together a list of the ten least important or most time-consuming things you do. You now have four options as to how to deal with them:

- Delete them: immediately stop things that are not important

- Delegate them: pass them to someone else, not necessarily someone working for you.

- Do them better: for example, if you have a two-hour project review meeting, think about how you could complete it in one hour or even a half hour.

- Defer them: in other words, identify activities that aren't such a priority. Be careful not to defer Quadrant 2 activities, though.

5. **In with the New:** Highlight some new areas to emphasize. These will include your own ideas to change your Quadrant 1/Quadrant 2 balance, plus some new leadership opportunities. Our research suggests that leadership opportunities for IT managers fall into one of ten categories, as shown in Figure 2. To help you along, there is a list of leadership opportunities in Chapter 6. This list has been compiled over a period of time from IT managers in all industries working around the world and includes opportunities from both *Excellent IT Management* and *Excellent IT Leadership*.

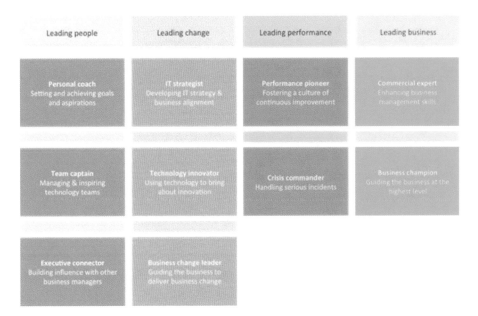

FIGURE 2. LEADERSHIP SKILLS AND AREAS OF OPPORTUNITY

1.6 CREATE YOUR OWN BRAND

As IT managers make the transition from management to leadership, they find some interesting changes start to happen in how they view the world. Their decision paradigm changes, their outlook changes, and so do their actions. They start to make decisions based on what is right for their organization rather than what is right for them personally. Decisions are based on a new paradigm, one where the success of their organization is their responsibility. It is no longer possible for them to be successful and their organization (either the IT organization or the corporate organization) not to be. They start to see financial decisions requiring capital investment or budget management as spending their own money. It is a good time to set new and exacting standards, not least because if bad habits are allowed to continue, they can be difficult to stop.

In this case, it is important to choose the right battles. Staff members who are often a few minutes late at the beginning of the day but more than work their hours would not be a good target. On the other hand, if poor timekeeping is starting to creep in at both ends of the day, it might be worth organizing team meetings to start at the beginning of the day.

Leadership is a two-way street. Demanding more from your team is one thing, but your team will also expect high leadership standards from you in return—in particular, they need you to be trustworthy and reliable. So, now is the time to think about your own personal brand. When you go to the supermarket, you expect certain standards from the goods you buy there. Food companies spend billions reminding you of this. As an IT executive moves from management to leadership, branding becomes important.

1.6.1 Product Packaging

When we think of food brands or clothing brands, at the simplest level, we think of product design and packaging, The color of the packaging, the packaging label, and materials, as well as the product itself.

Packaging is important. It can help to differentiate two products with similar characteristics. How many of us have chosen a product off the supermarket shelf based on the packaging design? I did exactly that a few days ago, choosing coffee based purely on its expensive-looking design. I made the irrational but completely normal leap that a company able to design nice packaging must also make good coffee!

In the same way, but without taking the analogy too far, we need to package ourselves effectively. The way we dress, personal grooming, the way we speak, our body language, the office we work in, the tidiness of our desk, the pictures on our wall, the car we drive, to name a few, all of these make up the brand that everyone around us sees. A strong brand is necessary for people to buy into your leadership.

It is important to recognize also that it is the accumulation of all these characteristics that give the overall impression and are the most important aspects of people's first impression of you. I had a situation a couple of years ago, where I was working with a colleague. He had had trouble finding the client's office and came into the meeting room ten minutes late, wearing an old coat and carrying a scruffy backpack. He happened to be one of the leading experts in his field, but it took over an hour into the meeting before the client realized his true talent. And not all are so open-minded. Many people make a first impression and stay with it.

One manager we were coaching took what we were talking about with regard to personal branding to evaluate what clues he may be giving away. He had always carried a screwdriver in his top pocket, a carryover from his days as a senior technician, where he always wanted to show his hands-on approach to solving problems What he came to realize was that this branded him as a techie, rather than a business executive. He had been a business manager for some years. He felt like a business manager, but for the first time, he came to realize that he was giving out the wrong messages.

The accumulation effect of the different brand "tells"[7] is important, but how we combine the different factors is not straightforward. It only requires one negative tell or one bad habit to undo all the good work. One unprompted outburst or patronizing comment can be all it takes. Or, it might be an interview candidate dressed in their nicest interview outfit, only to be let down by scuffed shoes.

1.6.2 Branded by Our Actions

The physical aspects of our appearance are important for first impressions. Fortunately, most IT managers work with the same people over a long period of time. They can expect that our business peers, sponsors, and users will really get to know them properly. In most cases, therefore, personality becomes much more important than the initial brand tells.

As we transition from management to leadership, we need to give this some active consideration. In particular, how do we want people to see us? Do we want to be seen as a hard taskmaster? Do we want to be seen as very helpful? Do we want to be seen as an innovator and a pioneer? So, now it gets interesting. To get to an answer, you need to know who you are. You need to know what you stand for. You need to know your values. And that may mean asking some harsh questions and being honest in the answers. You may want to be seen as caring, but if you have a very competitive or aggressive nature, this is unlikely to happen. Your values represent your character, and your character is what will allow others to trust you. It is a very important principle of leadership that you will only be trusted if others fully believe that the character they see is your true character. Your trustworthiness, the ability for others to trust you, means that you are acting out what you believe in. It may be possible from time to time to put on an act and hide your true character. But to be a successful leader, you must know what you stand for. You need to be consistent. Most important of all, you need to be trustworthy.

---

7 A "tell" is an expression from gambling that refers to the individual giveaway habits of fellow card players.

1.6.3 Quality of the Goods and Service

For many of us, it seems extraordinary that the money invested in brand-ing could possibly payoff, but it does. It invokes positive feelings in our decision, and most importantly, it invokes trust. When we see our favorite brand of soda, with all its associated colors and packaging, we know that this will be the same as the last one we bought. The taste, that attention to quality, and so on. That is why we pay more for a brand we recognize.

So, in building our brand, we need to consider quality. That means setting some quality standards and staying with them. It means delivering consistently to these high standards. Those who work for us also need to be very clear what it is that we stand for. And we must lead by example. It could be something as simple as time-keeping. If this is something impor-tant to us, and we adhere to our own standards, others will follow. One of the consequences of transitioning from management to leadership is that we become *completely* dependent on the standards, the quality of work, and the success of those who work for us. The role of leadership is primarily one of inspiration, guiding, and empowering. Our role becomes much less one of actually doing. And that is probably the hardest transi-tion of all.

1.6.4 An exercise in Building Our Own Brand

The following is a simple exercise that may help you in mapping your own brand.

What are my values?
So, what do you stand for? It may take several rounds to get to a set of values that you feel represent you. Different questions might help reveal interesting aspects as to what you find important and what is unimport-ant. Examples of questions you may wish to ask yourself include:

1. What are the things that I consider very important?

2. What are the character traits of those I admire the most?

3. What are the character traits I do not like in others?

4. What are the values of my organization (and do I really believe in them)?

5. Are there other beliefs that guide me (e.g., religious beliefs), and which of these are the most important?

Generally, when you first do this, the list grows and grows. To really get to the heart of what is important to you, you will probably need to rank the values in order and choose the most relevant.

What are my greatest and most enjoyable achievements?
A certain amount of reflection is needed for this part. You can consider your greatest achievements from all aspects of your life. Generally, we feel a good deal of pride and satisfaction in these achievements. But it is possible that you only look back on them with pride because they are behind you. Consider someone who ran a marathon for the first time for charity. They may have never run anything like the distance before, and perhaps they had never enjoyed running before and certainly aren't planning another anytime soon! So, they may consider it a great achievement, but it would not be a relevant achievement in the creation of a brand because it is something they did not particularly enjoy.

This exercise will also help you understand what the right conditions are for you to thrive. If all your greatest (work) achievements were for a previous company that had different structures, processes, and motivations, you might want to ask yourself, "What do I need to realize similar successes in my current post?" And what are the options, if these are not easily achievable? It is not uncommon for successful managers to need a particular type of boss to succeed. In coaching sessions, I have heard many coachees complain that their potential is being stifled because their bosses are micromanaging them. In these cases, they need to get out and find a more rewarding environment.

What are my strengths?

The objective here is to verify that the strengths you think you have are supported by hard evidence. Our strengths are important in the context of brand. It is difficult from a nontechnical person to promote themselves as a technologist if they are not technical (although, I have seen it done!) If you promote yourself as an innovator, a good track record of innovation and a talent for creativity helps. Remember, your strengths are probably those skills you need when you are most enjoying your work. The sort of strengths that IT people major in include:

1. Systems architectural design
2. Team motivation
3. Creativity
4. Business understanding
5. Relationship management
6. Financial awareness
7. Vendor management
8. System design
9. IT strategy
10. Project management
11. Technical problem resolution
12. Crisis handling

And so on. Think about your top five strengths. Some may come from the list above, some may come from previous jobs, and some should come from your current work.

What are the benefits of my brand?

Looking at the three aspects of value, achievements, and strengths, you can start to identify what your brand should mean to others. What can they expect from you when they work with you? In the same way we talked about the quality and consequent benefits of clothing or food brands, what are the key things that you will always offer? How does your experience, for example, of working abroad translate into how you

will help others in your current organization? Examples of benefits we have heard at this stage include:

1. A timely response to requests
2. Take time to understand the real problem
3. Recognize cultural/personality differences
4. A rational approach to problem solving
5. It will be fun and interesting
6. You will keep ownership but be coached for success
7. It will be carefully thought through and structured
8. The technical design will be accurate and use best in-class solutions
9. We will evaluate different options and not jump to conclusions
10. It will avoid the pitfalls of sourcing agreements of the past

Identify three of four benefits that people who work with you will gain.

What sort of person are you?

Having spent some time thinking about values and your key strengths, think how you would summarize what sort of person you are. Think about what sort of person you want to be, what sort of person you are most likely to become. What would give you the most satisfaction? If you enjoy doing something, it feels a lot less like work, and you will focus more completely on it. This may sound a bit too idealistic to be practical. If this is how you are thinking, you may also need to think about who your "target market" is. Who are the most important people who will be "buying" your brand? Typically, this includes your boss, other senior managers, and board members, and it may include influential figures in your marketplace outside your organization.

Some examples of summarized brand statements from other IT managers include:

1. Technologist—understanding the latest technologies in the marketplace

2. Business Person—the ability to look at what IT means in terms of business (revenue and costs)

3. Problem Solver—a rational approach to solve any problem

4. Crisis Manager—the person who likes an urgent problem that requires a calm head and quick decision making

5. Facilitator—someone who knows everyone and can put people together for the common good

6. Diplomat—someone who soothes tensions and resolves problems that arise between different factions

7. Strategist—someone who is able to look at options for the future and create a plan to meet long-term aims

8. Inspired Change Leader—the ability to guide an organization through difficult change, inspiring and motivating people to achieve their best

9. Innovator—the ability to understand new technologies and identify opportunities for them

10. Coach/Mentor—someone who coaches and develops people to the best of their ability

You may also feel that your brand represents more than one of these. In fact, some managers have four or five key roles in their overall brand. Any more is probably inadvisable, as an important aspect of brand is to really focus it on the key attributes and tailor it for the most important audiences.

The benefits and outcomes

As you develop your ideas on what sort of person you are, what your strengths really are, and the "promise of your brand," think about how

well you match up to this image. What are the things you do well that promote your brand to others? Are there things you do that detract from this brand? What would others say about your brand? As a final activity, put together a list of actions that will help to enhance your brand and reinforce it with your key stakeholders.

1.7 MAKE YOUR CHANGES COUNT

For an objective to really succeed, it needs some careful thought. It needs a "well-formed outcome," a concept that comes from the world of neurolinguistic programming (NLP).[8] The idea is to think carefully about the desired outcome of an objective. From this, we can put some steps in place to achieve what we really want.

There are four stages that need to be followed:

1. State your desired outcome in a positive way. For example, let us suppose that you are looking to build influence with a new department within the business. Just saying that you want to get to know these people better is not specific enough. Get to the heart of *why* you want to meet them. The outcome needs to be stated in positive terms; for example, "I want to get to know the new department to improve the quality of the systems that IT delivers to them and get earlier visibility of problems."

2. List the steps you will take to achieve the goal. In this example, you may wish to put together a relationship campaign, identify the key players, work out how to approach each one, how best to build rapport, and so on.

3. Think about if this is going to be a win-win for everyone. So, in our example, spending an hour a day with the new department's managers might help you to know them better, but it may not build credibility or be a good use of your time or theirs. If the primary

---

8 Sue Knight, *NLP at Work, the Essence of Excellence*, (2009).

goal is to improve the quality of the systems, consider exactly how the new department perceives value and make this the key theme of the relationship building.

4. Finally, check that your well-formed outcome fits with who you are and that you are willing to pay the price. This is a sense check at the end of the assessment that the objective is valuable, the plan is realistic, and that the actions are ones that you are comfortable and authorized to pursue.

This simple process encourages you to think about the desired outcome. By working through how to get there, it makes the outcome much more likely to be achieved. Think about how you could apply the "well-formed outcome," thinking about your key business and personal objectives.

COLLECT YOUR THOUGHTS

Use the form below to improve your time profile. Start with your objectives and your important tasks today. Put together a list of things to stop or do less of. Add some new Quadrant 2—or leadership—opportunities.

	Five Key Objectives	
	Five Important Things You Do	
	Five Things to Stop or Reduce	
	Five New Things	

TABLE 3. COLLECT YOUR THOUGHTS

2. Team Leadership

IN THIS CHAPTER, WE DISCUSS WHAT MAKES A GOOD IT TEAM. THE OBJEC-
TIVE IS TO HELP YOU THINK ABOUT HOW YOU CURRENTLY RUN YOUR
team and offer some new ideas. As an IT manager, you probably already
recognize that leading technology teams requires particular skills and expertise. Technology teams have their own characteristics. For example, most IT
team members are highly trained and often have a technical degree. But
strongly developed, highly logical minds can also create their own problems!
IT employees often believe that technical knowledge is of the utmost importance and a very good measure of ability. And they are sometimes surprised
to see how highly companies value employees who have limited technical
understanding.

IT people are often self-sufficient. This is a good thing, but it can reduce
the communication among team members. They also love solving problems,
and they are often on the lookout for problems to solve. Unfortunately, this
can appear very negative to outsiders. Observations of IT staff also suggest
that they may find it difficult to work in a hierarchical organization and to take
instruction, particularly if their managers are not technical. Team managers,
therefore, need to be more inclusive in their approach, think carefully about
how work is allocated, and recognize the importance of good technical skills.

In summary, there are some real differences in the makeup of technology
teams compared to other company departments. Here are our top guidelines
for managing IT teams. There will almost certainly be some overlap between
our guidelines and your experience but hopefully some useful, new ideas, too.

2.1 RECRUIT GOOD PEOPLE

The team you inherit won't be perfect, but that's all the more reason to make the most of any opportunity that presents itself to take on new people. Use these opportunities wisely, and follow these guidelines:

- If possible, ask for the right to hire one or two people onto your team when you take the job. Ideally, you should be looking to bring in one or two managers with you've worked with in the past.

- If you do need to hire from outside, and you do not have a candidate readily available, choose a good recruitment firm or headhunter. Work with them to choose the best candidates. Pay attention to the style, layout, and ordering of their CVs. It tells you a lot about the candidates, how they view themselves and their achievements. Look at more, rather than fewer CVs. It will take you only one minute to scan a CV, if you know what you are looking for. Recruitment opportunities are too important to waste.

- Be clear what you are asking for, but don't be too specific. The skills you need today may well change in a few weeks. You may regret it if you choose a specialist who can't adapt. Good people will be versatile.

- Always conduct your interviews with a colleague, ideally your HR manager. It will serve you well in terms of speeding things up, getting a second opinion on candidates, and keeping you tuned in to a group that generally knows everything that is going on. HR will understand the procedural side of interviewing, as well as the legal aspects, such as age, sex, and racial discrimination laws. They will probably have a better understanding of market pay rates, as well. In short, they will help you find better people quicker.

- Think about what competencies are required for the role. "Competency interviews" are used quite frequently these days. Here, every interview is conducted in the same way with the same questions to test for the specific competencies required for the job. When you are recruiting technical people, test their technical knowledge thoroughly (i.e., don't take their word that they are competent, just because they did it in their last job.) All the major blue chip companies that I work with require candidates to take a written test whenever technical knowledge is required. Remember that competence is not the same as personality, so test for that, too. Research shows that "gut feel" can also be a valuable tool[9] in choosing the right candidate. One IT director we work with asks one of his direct reports to take any potential candidate out for lunch. The resulting feedback tells him a lot about how the candidate would fit in.

- Prepare properly for interviewing candidates. There is nothing more certain to put off qualified candidates than an interviewer who doesn't know their name or hasn't read their CV. Less qualified candidates will not be put off, so lack of preparation is one of the best ways to ensure you get poor candidates.

- Put candidates at ease—you are recruiting them to do a job in the IT department, not to be good in high-pressure interviews. Ask them what they know about your company, and listen carefully to their answer. Of course, knowing about your company isn't the same as being able to do the job, but at least you will know they have done their research and are interested. There is no greater mistake than recruiting someone who can do the job but doesn't want to.

- As the interviewer, take care not to talk too much in the interview. Studies show that interviewers rate candidates higher in proportion to how much the interviewer talks, so take care not to be misled by someone who managed to keep you talking but is not suitable.

- It can take time to find the right people. Don't be tempted to give in to deadlines. If you are in doubt, keep looking. It would be a crying shame to fill a rare vacancy with the wrong person.

---

9 Malcolm Gladwell, *Blink*, (2006).

3.1 IT ORGANIZATION

3.1.1 Organizational Structures

Good organization for the overall IT department is vital. Many options and permutations exist and include the following or a combination of the following:

- Life cycle (e.g., strategy and planning, projects, application support, infrastructure)

- Process (e.g., sales process, manufacturing process)

- Departmental (e.g., sales department, distribution)

- Location (e.g., Europe, Asia, North America)

- Application (e.g., ERP, CRM)

The ideal structure depends on the topology of the organization, but a structure with a department each for planning, projects, service desk, and infrastructure, plus application support mirroring the business units, is usually a good starting point. Set up your reporting lines carefully. Typically, a manager will have between five and nine reports. Recognize that there is no perfect solution, and the most difficult problems need to be placed with your best managers.

Think about the flow of information among your team members. Each overlap is a potential problem, where they will need to come to you for resolution. If possible, put people with similar skill sets in the same areas to help with resource allocation. Keep the project list manageable to keep the department working effectively. Give consideration as to how the organization appears to the rest of the business. Points of contact should be clear, and if your business relationship managers promise something to the business users, they should have the authority to deliver it.

3.1.2 Clear Roles and Responsibilities

A key part of organizational management is the development of the right skills and deploying them to best effect. The Skills Framework for the Information Age (SFIA)[10] provides a clear, universally recognized model for describing an IT practitioner's skills. They are defined in two axes:

- **Categories**—which are further broken down into subcategories to group standard IT job roles

- **Levels**—which define the different levels of competence or attainment

SFIA does not define the categories or subcategories. It defines only the skills. The categories and subcategories are merely a way of organizing the skills on paper. So, the categories and subcategories might change according to your organization. Clearly, there are also behavioral skills, (which some people refer to as "soft skills"), but SFIA deals with what we refer to as "professional skills."

SFIA Categories	SFIA Levels
Strategy and architecture	7. Set strategy/inspire, mobilize
Business change	6. Initiate/influence
Solution development and implementation	5. Ensure/advise
Service management	4. Enable

10 "Skills Framework for the Information Age (SFIA)," www.sfia.org.uk. SFIA is the intellectual property of the SFIA Foundation, a not-for-profit organization that distributes SFIA free of charge to end users.

Procurement and management support	3. Apply
Client interface	2. Assist
	1. Follow

TABLES 4A AND 4B. SFIA CATEGORIES AND LEVELS

The resulting matrix of these two axes shows the complete set of skills used by IT practitioners. SFIA provides an overall description for each skill, supported by a description of how the skill appears at each level of competency at which it is recognized.

2.2 CREATE HARMONY

Top teams work together in a particular and distinct way and normally have a set of team values to guide them. Value statements reflect the actual beliefs of an organization and must be backed up with actions, so there is clear evidence that they are supported. They guide behavior and, in effect, define culture. For a team to work in harmony, this code is vital. There are five characteristics of particular importance for successful teambuilding.

Mutual Respect: This refers how people in the company interact with each other and the respect they show for everyone at all levels. In France, the tradition of shaking hands with your colleagues each morning is a great example that reinforces communication and demonstrates mutual respect. The military has long had a tradition of getting together briefly at eleven o'clock every morning for coffee. These rituals emphasize the core beliefs of mutual respect.

PLACES WHERE PEOPLE COULDN'T SAY WHAT THEY THOUGHT

In his book, *How NASA Builds Teams*,[11] Charlie Pellerin tells the story of the Hubble telescope. At the time, he was NASA's director of astrophysics. Although the launch was successful, it soon became apparent that there was a serious flaw in the mirror. Sometime later, the failure review board told Congress that the flawed mirror was down to a leadership problem. It transpired that the contractors had not forwarded the results of numerous tests, which might have identified the failings. When asked why not, they reported that they were "tired of the beatings." NASA had become so hostile to its contractors that they stopped reporting any technical problems.

Malcolm Gladwell, in his book *Outliers*,[12] tells the story of Korean Air, whose planes in the early 1990s were crashing at a rate seventeen times that of the industry average. In a typical accident, there are seven consecutive human errors. These are rarely errors of technical or flying know-how but errors of teamwork and communication. Investigators found that the captain's social status was so high that the junior officers could only communicate obliquely and deferentially. In one case, the captain was trying to land the plane in severe weather conditions. He had committed to a visual approach, and the navigator knew there was worse weather ahead. Rather than clearly state that they were heading into a highly dangerous situation with no backup plan, he said, "The radar can help us a lot." The captain was tired and not listening to the hidden meaning. Ten minutes later, the plane crashed.

Honesty and Trust: Lencioni,[13] in his work on dysfunctional teams, emphasized the importance of trust in a team. He showed how teams without trust get sucked into a downward spiral of resentment and poor performance. One potentially damaging threat is when the

11 Charles J. Pellerin, How NASA Builds Teams, (2009).

12 Malcolm Gladwell, Outliers: The Story of Success, (2009).

13 Patrick Lencioni, *The Five Dysfunctions of a Team*, (2002).

organization is in competition with itself, with similar functions sitting in different departments. It is vital to spot such problems early. Reorganizing the fragmented functions often transforms teams very quickly. IT managers need to nurture and build a strong foundation of trust. Trust breeds cooperation from your team, which in turn breeds commitment, accountability, and attention to results. Your trust in your team will grow as a result, and so the positive spiral of trust becomes a self-fulfilling prophecy.

Pride and a Sense of Belonging: This is shown in how a company works together and the emphasis it places on teamwork; for example, the importance of keeping commitments and supporting other team members. Many organizations foster a sense of belonging through their values and often a dress code. For example, some companies have a special company uniform, whereas others are more relaxed with "Casual Fridays." These codes represent the culture of a company; what works for one company may not work for another.

Commitment and Loyalty: Any successful company must foster pride in hard work to remain successful, and at the heart of this is the commitment to the customer. Leading customer care is the job of everyone, not just those in direct contact with the customer. Objectives need to be set so that everyone shares in the company's commitment to quality and customer care.

Attitude toward Risk-Taking: An organization needs to know where it stands in terms of innovation and risk. Is it conservative, or does it like to be cutting edge? It is all very well for a company to say they encourage risk-taking and innovation. The test comes when something goes wrong—does the management team stay supportive?

INTERNATIONAL TEAMS: DIPLOMATIC RELATIONS

In today's IT world, more and more teams are international in nature. Understanding the different outlooks of different cultures is an increasingly vital skill for IT managers. In collaboration with a number of international CIOs, we have put together this list of six guidelines for working across international and cultural boundaries.

1. **Be easy to understand**. Those who are native or fluent English speakers are fortunate that English is the international language of business. But even though it is second nature for you, be patient with those who are not natural English speakers. It is important that you speak clearly, which generally also means slowly. Use short sentences and simple grammatical structures, and avoid long words and slang expressions.

2. **Write down important instructions**. One technique that worked well for the CIO of a large technology company was to write detailed e-mails, explaining instructions and providing guidance for key activities at critical times. E-mail allows words to be fine-tuned, making the meaning clear and unambiguous. Colleagues can also refer back to it.

3. **Really take time to listen**. I mean, really listen. It may mean long pauses in the conversation while colleagues are trying to find the right words to express themselves. You should never attempt to finish someone's sentence. Pay attention, and don't interrupt.

4. **Recognize that your way isn't necessarily right**. And it certainly isn't the only way. Different countries approach problems in different ways. Just because something worked for you in your country doesn't mean it will work in another. Never underestimate the resourcefulness, intelligence, and expertise of the people you are working with. the middle

ground; in other words, take time to think of ideas that capture the best of everything from both sides—methods, experiences, and cultures. Indonesians have an expression, *gatong rayong*, which literally means "carrying together" and reflects the importance of colleagues working together on plans they have all signed up for.

5. **Be sensitive to culture and social context**. One of the most exciting and rewarding aspects of working in an international environment is the opportunity to learn about other cultures. Be sensitive to the fact that different cultures value different things. For example, so-called "high context" cultures, such as China and Korea, place a very high value on experience and seniority. Showing respect is essential in these environments. Always seek to learn about the way things are done. Be sensitive to everything and everyone around you, and adjust your behavior accordingly.

6. **Not all good news is good news**. Be aware that you may appear threatening to other cultures for any number of reasons. Show humility, and encourage your colleagues to come forward with problems without fear of criticism or reprimand. Many cultures do not like to give bad news and can—shall we say—distort the truth. A soft approach, demonstrating trustworthiness, is essential.

TABLE 5. DIPLOMATIC RELATIONS: GUIDELINES FOR INTERNATIONAL TEAMS

2.3 CREATING A BALANCE OF SKILLS

It is important to hire good people with the right skills, but this alone will not guarantee success. We also need the right balance of skills. To use the analogy of football or hockey, you would not want a team where everyone wants to be scoring goals—you need everyone to work closely together but focusing on their own job. Dr. Meredith Belbin[14] conducted extensive research on the subject of teams and developed a simple and practical model.

His research identified that every successful team needs skills in nine areas and that there should be someone to fill each of these nine roles or functions, or problems will occur. Since many teams have less than nine

14 Meredith Belbin, *Team Roles at Work*, (2010).

members, team members will often fulfill more than one role. However, unlike a psychometric profile, it is relatively easy to take on a different role if circumstances require. To assess your team roles, go to the Belbin website at www.belbin.com. For a relatively small cost, you can complete the online survey for yourself or, better still, for your whole team. There is also some free resource material to accompany the team role tests.

THE NINE BELBIN ROLES

PLANT: Creative, imaginative, and unorthodox. Solves difficult problems.

RESOURCE INVESTIGATOR: Extroverted, enthusiastic, and communicative. Explores opportunities. Develops contacts.

COORDINATOR: Mature, confident, and trusting. A good chairperson. Clarifies goals, promotes decision-making.

SHAPER: Dynamic, outgoing, and high-strung. Challenges, pressurizes, finds ways around obstacles. Reviews progress of the project and gives energy/redirection as necessary.

MONITOR/EVALUATOR: Sober, strategic, and discerning. Sees all options and has a reputation for making accurate judgments.

TEAM WORKERS: Sociable, perceptive, and accommodating. Listens to what is going on and can sense when things are not right. Good diplomats and can avert difficult situations.

IMPLEMENTER: Disciplined, reliable, conservative, and efficient. Turns ideas into practical action.

COMPLETER/FINISHER: Painstaking, conscientious, and often anxious. Searches out errors and omissions and makes sure the project delivers a good level of quality.

SPECIALIST: Single-minded, self-starting, and dedicated. Provides knowledge or technical skills that are in rare supply.

TABLE 6. BELBIN ROLES

Team members generally fulfill their roles at all times, but some really come into their own during particular stages of a project. At the outset, a project needs the ideas person—the plant, in Belbin terms. Of course, not all ideas are good ideas, so the monitor/evaluator is needed to select the best ones. Once the project is under way, you need a project manager, usually fulfilled by the coordinator, and someone to find the resources—the resource investigator. Next, the work of the implementer and team worker begins, and the project makes progress. From time to time, it will be necessary for the shaper to look at things from a high level and redirect the project if required. As the project nears completion, the skills of the completer/finisher come into play to ensure that the product is delivered to a high standard of quality.

It is important to have expertise in different roles. Celebrate diversity in your team. Teams with lots of implementers implement lots of projects but not necessarily the right ones. We often find lots of implementers and quite a few shapers among IT managers but—it has to be said—not many plants.

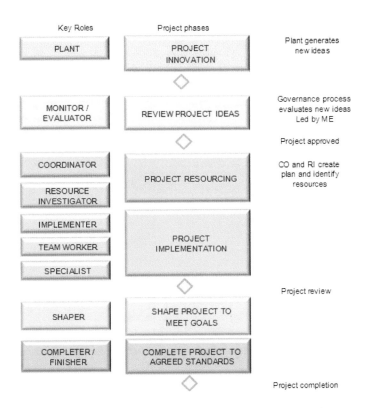

FIGURE 3. THE CHANGING EMPHASIS OF ROLES IN A PROJECT

2.4 SET DIRECTION AND OBJECTIVES

Good direction and clear objectives have a massive positive effect on the success of any team. Estimates suggest that performance can be increased by 20 percent with good, well-thought-through targets. Management books talk about vision as being an essential ingredient, and so it is. But vision also needs some reality sprinkled in, particularly for IT people. IT strategy should describe both your vision and the actual targets you are seeking to achieve.

As described by Kaplan and Norton[15] in their book *The Balanced Scorecard*, objectives should be set in each of the four quadrants of the balanced scorecard, namely customer or end-user objectives (in the case of IT); process objectives,

---

15 Kaplan and Norton, *The Balanced Scorecard, Translating Strategy into Action* (1996).

including technical performance (again, in the case of IT); people objectives; and financial objectives.

From the IT objectives, define objectives for every IT team member. Objectives should be properly defined using the SMART acronym, as follows:

- **S**pecific—clearly defined and unambiguous

- **M**easurable—in terms of time, cost, quantity, and/or quality

- **A**chievable—in other words, agreed to and understood by the team member

- **R**ealistic—the necessary resources available, enough time has been allocated, and there are no conflicting tasks

- **T**imely—a clear timetable is agreed upon

All objectives should have a line of sight, where there is a clear link from the top-level goals of the CEO, through the departmental objectives of IT, to the individual objectives of every team member. The following three questions will help assess if a team is heading in a good direction:

1. Does the team know what to do?

2. Does the team know when to do it?

3. Does the team know in what order to do it?

Objectives should have a baseline—which is the minimum level to be achieved—and a stretch target. Stretch targets can be an enormous source of motivation, allowing team members to prove that they can do more than just their job description.

2.5 CREATE A GOOD WORKING ENVIRONMENT

The more we've worked with IT teams, the more we've come to realize the importance of a good office environment. No two companies are the same, and what works for one may not work for another. Yet, too few IT departments think carefully about what is required or what could be improved. Office space is particularly important for IT staff, as they are more likely to be doing their work at their desks, rather than out on the road, visiting customers, for example. Breakout areas, where teams can discuss issues spontaneously, are vital.

AHMED'S STORY: WHERE HAVE ALL MY STAFF GONE?

I was working in a hospital, running a team of IT staff. We had been based in a new annex, but it was undergoing some renovation. In the meantime, we were moved back to the main building, into the basement. It was just like a scene out of the TV program *The IT Crowd.* There was no natural light, and the corridors were used as a storage area. The whole mood of the team changed. We lost 30 percent of our staff in six months. As their manager, I thought my job was to keep them motivated and persuade them to stay. It was only after four or five months that I realized I was putting my energy in the wrong place. I should have been fighting for better conditions, not appeasing my staff. I spoke to the CEO and found us two temporary locations above ground. It was still another six months before we moved back to our original refurbished office, but at least we didn't lose any more staff. It made me realize that you *can* change your working conditions if you put your mind to it, and your team will really respect you as a result.

The working environment includes many things, such as:

- location and access of the office to public transport or parking;

- location relative to other departments, for example, in the same building or on the same campus;

- the quality of the office decor, including furniture, and other office facilities, such as printers and copiers;

- working conditions, such as air conditioning and lighting;

- a proper reception area and enough meeting rooms;

- and additional facilities, such as breakout areas, quiet rooms, vending machines, cafeterias, and gyms.

Changing the working environment really does make a major difference in productivity. Think about your working environment. It is easy to think that it is the responsibility of the facilities manager or someone else, but it is surprising what you can achieve with a little application.

Finally, the rest of the organization is looking to you to create good, easy-to-use IT. Some of this comes down to ergonomics and the physical environment. IT managers should work with HR to make sure screens are well-maintained and large enough for the task, attention is given to prevention of RSI (repetitive strain injuries) with good design, laptops are easily portable, and chairs are comfortable. Options such as thin client desktop computers are ideal for reducing office noise—it is easy to forget how noisy work environments can become.

2.6 DEVELOP SKILLS

In the world of IT, it is important to keep abreast of new technical developments and keep skills relevant. IT managers have a duty to develop their team. Here are some ideas that will help.

2.6.1 Delegate and Coach

All managers need to delegate to get their job done. But the way in which managers delegate says a lot about their effectiveness. It also provides a great opportunity for developing team skills. Use different styles in different situations.[16] For example, for new, inexperienced team members, act as a teacher, providing clear instructions for what needs to be done and how to best go about doing it. For more experienced team members, act as their coach. Outline what needs to be done, and guide them to the right approach. For experienced managers, give a high-level view of what is required, and make yourself available to act as a sounding board if needed.

Coaching is not a simple exercise, but it can be a highly effective way to develop the skills of your team. It can be done formally, through regular progress reviews, or informally, taking advantage of opportunities in the day-to-day working environment. This book is too short to discuss coaching in depth, but I have found the book *Masterful Coaching*[17] helpful. A key component of delegation and coaching is providing effective feedback. According to a recent survey, 70 percent of managers are either unable or unwilling to have the courageous feedback conversation needed to address the developmental need of staff. Twenty percent are unable to have the conversation without using an aggressive or confronting style, which means only 10 percent are actually having conversations with a purpose and in a style that works. It is a vital and valuable tool. The following chart describing the GROW model of feedback may help you.

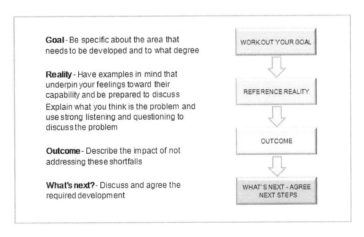

FIGURE 4. THE GROW MODEL—FOUR STEPS TO GIVING GOOD FEEDBACK

---

16 Hersey, Blanchard, and Johnson, *Management & Organizational Behaviour*, (1996).

17 Hargrove, *Masterful Coaching*, (2008).

2.6.2 Team Meetings

Regular IT team meetings are the ideal opportunity to develop skills. To avoid overlap with day-to-day issues, schedule an additional half day of development every two or three months. Allocate the time early, and choose the topics. Consider inviting the managing director to talk about plans for the future or the marketing director to talk about new products. Alternatively, ask a team member, industry expert, or external training company to run the session. Make them interactive—listening to presentations for four hours rarely makes for an interesting or productive afternoon.

2.6.3 Business Meetings

Normal business meetings are also a great way to develop team skills. When I worked as a sales account manager many years ago, I learned a lot about the value of pre-meeting preparation. Once a month, I would be required to book an appointment with my manager. As I drove to the client, he would ask me a multitude of questions about the meeting objectives, the personalities who would be there, potential problems that might occur, and so on. This preparation made an extraordinary difference to the meeting success and was a fantastic learning experience for me.

If one of your team members is running the meeting, spend ten minutes or so with them beforehand and quiz them about what the meeting is for and the desired outcomes. Ask them what role they would like you to play, and identify a couple of development areas to focus on. Typical objectives you may set might include:

- Build rapport: look to set up new opportunities to get to know peers and senior managers better

- Build credibility: for example, with a key sponsor or business user

- Understand problems better: for example, using advanced questioning techniques

- Find out what is happening in the organization: learn more about products, senior-level strategy, and such

Working with your team members on a one-to-one basis helps in many other ways. You will develop your unspoken set of rules and better manage the discussions. For example, while one asks the questions, the other can be listening carefully and preparing questions to find out more. It is a great way to empower your team. One CIO of a large hotel chain said that if he was in a meeting with one of his team, he would never run the meeting himself. He would position himself as a senior representative who could arbitrate on issues as they arose.

2.6.4 Training Courses

An obvious way to develop IT management and technical skills quickly is through a training program. It would be remiss of me not to mention my company, IT Leaders. We run accredited public, in-house, and distance learning courses all around the world based on this book and *Excellent IT Management*.

What I would say, though, is whichever course you choose, the value that experienced managers gain from working with other delegates from all over the world in every industry is immense—far greater than attending a generic leadership course. Our delegates also benefit from being part of our international IT manager network. This, as with any other peer network, provides a great opportunity for asking opinions on IT matters at any time.

Other valuable IT training includes IT process training, such as PRINCE II, ITIL, and more technical courses. Even if this is not a prerequisite for your job, a foundation course on the key process models is helpful for running any significant IT team.

2.6.5 Use Vendors and Networks

Leading vendors offer an excellent insight into the IT industry. They work for many organizations at a time, and they know the market and the latest technology intimately. Many produce white papers and journal articles. They know what the future of the industry will bring because they are already working on the next generation of products. It is worth asking your account managers to bring in their senior architects and marketing directors to update you on the latest trends and innovations.

External consultants can also help to develop skills. If you are about to commission a new consulting assignment, allocate one of your IT team members to the consulting team to retain the knowledge in house. Examples of such assignments might include developing strategic plans, creating a manual of IT standards, or evaluating supplier spending.

2.6.6 Networking

There are many networking groups set up for IT managers, including our own IT Leaders Network, which meets three times a year. Networking is not just about joining network groups. It is important for all IT managers to build a close group of peers, associates, and colleagues they can confide in. This is easier said than done, and it takes time and a concerted, proactive effort to achieve.

2.7 MANAGE PERFORMANCE

So far, we have talked about the straightforward management aspects of recruiting and developing your team. But what if you have a problem with one of your team members? In this case, you will need to think carefully about how to resolve it. A good starting point is to review how it came about. You will find, though, that most problems are down to management. To assess if this is the case, ask the following three questions:

- Does the team member have the skills they need to do the job and, if not, why not? Is it a problem with recruitment, or are they in a role that doesn't suit them?

- Is their poor performance down to external factors (e.g., personal problems) or an attitude tarnished by previous bad management?

- Are they doing an impossible task? Perhaps the job is undoable because of inadequate resources or the wrong contractors. Is it caused by a root problem with procurement?

If you know you need to make a staff change, then act quickly. Be tough and focused. Notify HR at the earliest opportunity, and don't stop until the problem is resolved. It is important to work with experienced HR staff. Junior HR staff often spend too long trying to turn poor performers around. Worse still, they excuse their behavior and refuse to act. Work only with tough HR managers with the courage to exit problem employees—don't let your organization be a haven for poor performers!

DIETER'S STORY: ACT NOW WITH DISRUPTIVE PEOPLE

I had just joined a new company as their CIO. I soon found out that one of my direct reports had also applied for the job, but of course had not been successful. This person became very disruptive and was increasingly causing problems with the other managers. I chose to work with him for several weeks before the situation came to a head, and an agreement was made for him to leave. It was not that he was a bad person—just one in the wrong position. Once he had gone, the whole dynamic and productivity of the department transformed. It reminded me of when a car alarm goes off down the road. You don't realize how annoying it is until it stops. At first, I thought it would be too much hassle to sort it out, but, looking back, it would have been better all around if I had acted more quickly.

It is much easier to recruit good, high-quality people than to invest a lot of time in those who will never make the grade. This sounds harsh, but we shouldn't forget that poor performers are usually unhappy and unfulfilled in their work, and it often suits everyone to find them something

else to do. A poorly performing employee can really damage team morale and productivity. Jim Collins describes in his book *Good to Great*[18] that great companies still "churn" as many people as less successful companies. Churn is defined as staff turnover from employees moving to new jobs, retiring, or being fired (i.e., not from layoffs). It wasn't that they churned more or less; they churned better. So, people either stayed a long time or left sooner.

2.8 REWARDS AND RECOGNITION

Our final guideline for building strong teams relates to rewards, and in particular, rewarding the right behavior and matching actions to consequences. The process starts with the manager asking a team member to carry out a particular activity. Instinctively, the team member will want to know what is in it for him—what are the positive and negative consequences, and how can he influence those consequences?

Interestingly, actions and consequences often contradict each other. For example, you would expect that if a particular activity was performed well, there would be positive consequences for this. Similarly, if the activity was not performed well, there would be negative consequences. But, in fact, we often see that positive actions have negative consequences, and negative actions have positive ones.

A good example came from the customer care department of one of our clients. One incident manager was particularly good at handling difficult, awkward, and sometimes rude customers. So, you can probably guess that the reward he got for his skill was to spend all day handling difficult, awkward, and rude customers. If we do not give consideration to the link between the action and its consequence, we can unwittingly demoralize our team.

Rewards cover a wide range from a simple thank you to a job promotion and everything in between. Research published in a recent *McKinsey*

---

18 Jim Collins, *Good to Great*, (2001).

Quarterly[19] survey identified that praise from immediate managers, leadership attention (for example, one-on-one conversations), and a change to lead projects or task forces were no less or even more effective motivators than the three highest rated financial incentives, namely cash bonuses, increased base pay, or stock options.

Other examples for motivating and rewarding your team include:

- Dinner for employees and their partners

- On-the-spot awards (anything from $100 upward)

- Team awards

- "Freebies," such as T-shirts, thumb drives, and so on

- A research budget to try out new technologies

Finally, if your team has been successful, you need a way to celebrate. Team celebrations can sometimes be met with a groan from cynical team members, so plan them carefully. Technology teams can be different, and they may not see a reception—accompanied by a lot of strangers—as reward for anything. But if done in the right way, team celebrations are good opportunities to acknowledge the great work that a team has done, inspiring it to continue and grow.

---

19 "Motivating People, Getting Beyond Money," *McKinsey Quarterly*, June 2009.

3. Effective Networking

3.1 RELATIONSHIP CAMPAIGNS

SENIOR EXECUTIVES ESTIMATE THAT THEY SPEND UP TO 50 PERCENT OF THEIR TIME NETWORKING! OF COURSE, THIS DOES NOT MEAN THEY walk the corridors aimlessly, hoping to meet someone important to chat with. They see networking opportunities in their day-to-day work—in a project review meeting, say, or preparing a negotiation or at the start of a board meeting. They will not typically sit on their own in the coffee shop until the meeting is about to start or eat a sandwich at their desk. They are out and about, meeting with their network contacts, finding out about the changing priorities of the business, and sharing their views (influencing, if you like) on developments in IT.

To do this requires a good network to work with. Networks do not just happen by accident. They require careful planning. Our studies show that effective networks have good contacts at three levels of influence. The first circle includes your closest advisors and confidantes. It probably includes your direct reports and your boss, among others. You trust these people implicitly and would discuss with them any problems that were troubling you. The second circle of influence includes those people with whom you work regularly, and you probably know quite a lot about each of them. It is the third circle, though, that is the most interesting.

PLOT YOUR NETWORK

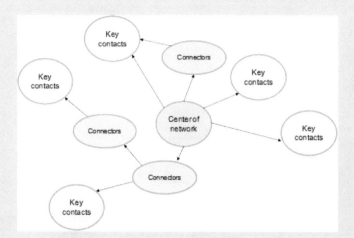

In putting your plan together, it is helpful to take a leaf out of the salesperson's book. The technique is called "strategic selling" and describes the importance of identifying key players and putting together an action plan to build influence. Use the five-step process below to identify key players who should be in your network of influence and build links to them.

1. Go through your address book, and choose thirty contacts you know reasonably well in different parts of your organization.

2. Link them together in a network diagram format showing how they connect to you and other managers (as demonstrated above).

3. Add five other influential managers you want to get to know better.

4. Identify the key connectors who connect them to you.

5. Put a plan together to get introduced to them (have something to talk about when you meet).

FIGURE 5. PLOT YOUR NETWORK

The third circle of influence contains those people you see from time to time. You meet them perhaps every four to six weeks, sometimes less. They will almost always work in different departments that you don't come into contact with that often. This group will often include the senior executives, influential sponsors, and probably your boss's boss. Unless you are on the board of directors, this group probably includes the CEO. The research consistently shows that it is this third group that holds the key for successful networkers.

THE IMPORTANCE OF NETWORKS: HOW IBM WAS TRANSFORMED

Although it happened in 1994, over twenty years ago, this story is as relevant as it ever was. IBM was the official technology sponsor of the Lillehammer Winter Olympics in Norway. But when David Grossman, a midlevel IBM manager, tried to find the Olympic results website, he found a rogue website run by Sun, using IBM's raw data feed. Eventually, IBM succeeded in shutting down the site. But the big problem was IBM's lack of awareness of what was going on in the new world of the Internet.

After the Olympics, Grossman hooked up a connection and showed IBM's head of marketing and a member of the strategy task force, John Patrick, what the Internet could do. From that point, Grossman was able to start an underground movement, mentored by Patrick. Patrick used his powerful network of contacts to open a lot of doors and build supporters, which soon included CEO Lou Gerstner. It was a classic case of the power of people networks to promote innovation and create energy for new ideas. It was the start of the revolution that enabled the Internet to become the major strategic thrust for the biggest computer company in the world.

From "Waking Up IBM: How a Gang of Unlikely Rebels Transformed IBM"[20] by Gary Hamel. To download the full article, go to http://explore.hbr.org.

---

20 Gary Hamel, "Waking Up IBM: How a Gang of Unlikely Rebels Transformed IBM," *Harvard Business Press,* July 2000.

Studies show that communication around an organization often passes through a small number of people. These are the key business networkers, sometimes called "connectors," the people whom everyone knows. Set yourself the target of becoming one of the networkers within your organization. There is no more certain way to ensure career success than a good network of contacts.[21]

At this point, it might be helpful to map your network to see if you are focusing too much on your first two circles of influence. Of course, it is not practical to drop everything to build influence further afield. Nonetheless, it is vital to create these opportunities. One thing we have noticed is that people with valuable networks invest time to keep in touch.

Here are seven guidelines for building effective networks:

1. Choose your friends—identify the people you need to know and gravitate toward people with energy, ideas, and humor. Avoid people who are always complaining and resistant to change. Remember, you can tell a lot about people by the company they keep.

2. Faire le point—in France, managers arrange to meet their peers and other senior managers on a regular basis. "Faire le point" translates roughly as a "regular catch up." These meetings typically take fifteen minutes. They have no formal agenda—just the intention of catching up with what is going on.

3. Be in the right places at the right time, sometimes known as "being visible." Typical events include project kickoffs, product launches, and financial performance updates.

4. Seek out opportunities for interaction, work closely with your boss, and build from his or her network.

5. Look for links with those you know in order to meet new people.

---

21 Malcolm Gladwell, *The Tipping Point*, (2001).

6. Get outside your comfort zone, and take calculated risks.

7. Seek to join the inner sanctum. This is the group of three or four people at the heart of any organization that holds the balance of power.

3.2 RAPPORT AND CREDIBILITY

Many IT managers find the relationship side of their work the most difficult. For some, working in a technical environment offers limited exposure to working with other managers outside the department. But it is such a vital skill that success is not an option. And the good news is that it is easier than you think. It just needs practice.

Building relationships starts with creating a good impression. We talked earlier about brand and how important it is to have a good professional brand. It makes those first encounters much easier. Even with a good brand reputation, though, first encounters can still be awkward. So, be prepared! Have something to say. Comedians often say that it takes a lot of practice to be spontaneous. So, do as they do, and prepare your lines beforehand. Like them, you may not know exactly what you are going to say, but the conversation will give prompts to something you have thought about already. Think about subjects of interest and common ground. Good subjects are often the market conditions, new product launches, or even carefully chosen current events. Whatever they are, have an opinion, but ask others what they think first.

In these situations, be observant. See who gets recognized and what they talk about. Keep on the lookout for opportunities to help. Be consistently polite, and return phone calls, answer e-mails, and meet deadlines. In short, keep your commitments. Don't whine to your coworkers about what is wrong. Bounce ideas around with them as to what a good solution might be. And, finally, treat every discussion with the business managers as an opportunity not to be missed.

Building rapport with business managers is the first step. But to get things done, every manager needs credibility. With credibility comes opportunity, and with opportunity comes success. Credibility is a key leadership attribute. It is the heart of business, and it is its most valuable weapon. Without it, failure is guaranteed. Credibility means that others believe and trust what you are saying and consequently seek your opinion. Table 7 shows seven guidelines that have helped other managers to build credibility with their peers.

CREDIBILITY GUIDELINES

1. Know your own company organization and the people you work with.
2. Have good sources of information, and quote them when appropriate.
3. Build a good track record.
4. Discuss concerns directly with people involved.
5. Be professional and speak calmly, accurately, and concisely.
6. Ask insightful questions, and encourage a response.
7. Listen to what people are saying.

TABLE 7. CREDIBILITY GUIDELINES

3.3 THE CLIENT'S VIEWPOINT

Day-to-day meetings are a perfect way to build relationships. And getting to know the requirements of your client is a vital part of this. Take time to understand what they are trying to do. Ask them about their priorities, and identify what is essential—"the needs"—and what is helpful (but not essential)—"the wants." Sometimes, IT managers hear the word "want" and assume it means "frivolous." It doesn't. Just because something is a "want" doesn't mean it isn't valuable. Imagine being given a smart phone today that doesn't do e-mail. Well, e-mail isn't *essential* on a phone—you have your PC for that! Emotional forces are often contained within the "want list," and delivering them may provide much needed energy and support to get a project completed.

IAN'S STORY: WHAT'S ON YOUR MIND?

I was the head of business relationship management for our Canadian division based in Montreal, having just moved from our US headquarters. I had been part of the design team that put together a corporate architecture using best-in-breed applications around an integration layer. It was a pretty neat solution, and we were keen for the Canadian subsidiary to adopt it.

Unfortunately, they didn't see things our way. As a recently acquired division, the business sponsors told me they were happy with what they had and didn't want some fancy (read: expensive) head office solution. The meetings became pretty heated.

Jennifer had just joined the company as the Canadian head of IT. What she did at the first meeting was amazing. Instead of talking about the US architecture, she asked them about their problems. What was keeping them up at night? As it turned out, quite a lot! She asked about the implications of this in terms of revenue lost, cost savings missed, quality, and so on. Before we knew it, they were starting to talk about the importance of replacing parts of the existing systems. Within a few months, some of the old systems had been replaced completely with modules from the new architecture. In fact, all the systems were replaced within just eighteen months.

Over a quiet drink one evening, Jennifer confided in me that she had used a technique called SPIN, [22] originally developed by Neil Rackham for the world of sales. The essence is to focus on user problems and their full business impact. It taught me a lot, especially how much we can learn from sales when working in business relationship management.

A technique used for understanding wants and needs is called "chunking up," a rather inelegant expression that means asking the

---

22 Neil Rackham, *SPIN Selling*, Gower Publishing, November, 1995.

business sponsors and users about their priorities and trying to get to the heart of what they really want. It tries to get behind the **feature** of what is desired (e.g., a large screen), in order to understand the underlying **benefit**. For example, a user might want a large screen because they need to see a lot of different information at the same time, which means they can handle customer queries better and so on. The feature is the screen size, the benefit is being able to see more information and handle queries better. The technique often repeats the key question, "Why?" in different forms; so, in our example, we might have asked, "So, why do you want that?" or "What will that get you?" and "How does that help?" to get to the real benefit of the original request for a large screen.

RICHARD MULLENDER—POLICE HOSTAGE NEGOTIATOR

At one of our recent IT networking events, we were fortunate to have invited a former police hostage negotiator, Richard Mullender. As someone who handled life-or-death situations every day of his working life, it is no surprise that his questioning and listening skills were extraordinary. He kindly gave us some insight into the most important communication skill, a process called *active listening*.

1. Use "minimal encouragers." These are the little words that we can use to keep people talking, such as "And?" or "Go on."

2. Summarize—this gives the other party a chance to say whether he agrees, or more likely, add further background.

3. Highlight and echo energy words—for example, "We really need this for March." Here, if you hear them emphasizing "March," then it means it is probably the main energy word. If you just echo this by saying, "For March?" the likelihood is the other party will tell you why.

4. Mirroring their posture makes you more like them. The more you are like them, they more they like you.

5. Label understanding—interpret in your own words what you heard them say. For example:

   - I feel as if…
   - I sense that…
   - It appears to me that…
   - It sounds to me like…
   - It seems to me that…

6. Listen from their point of view—not autobiographic, silent, combative, or conciliatory—but from their point of view.

From Richard Mullender, Cliff Edge Communications[23]

TABLE 8. ACTIVE LISTENING

---

23 Richard Mullender, *Communication Secrets of a Hostage Negotiator,* Griffin Professional Business & Training Services, 2012.

Guiding conversations with business sponsors is a vital skill for any business relationship manager. The use of smart questions is a hugely versatile technique. Here are some different types of questions to use at different times in your discussions.

1. Most people are familiar with open questions. These are ones that require an answer of more than one word. They are helpful in getting the other party talking. Examples might include, "How would you like this to work?" or "Do you have any suggestions as to how we might improve this for next time?"

2. The opposite of the open question is, logically enough, the closed question. This is one that requires a one-word answer. These are useful to get absolute clarity about the truth. For example, "Do you think this will be ready on Tuesday?" You often see journalists trying to pin down politicians with closed questions, demanding a single word response; for example, "Were you, or were you not, aware that this was going on?"

3. Probing questions are the next level up, and they require a certain amount of skill and sophistication. They invariably build upon the answer from a previous question that provides an opportunity to ask a secondary question. In effect, they are used to try to find out more about a particular situation.

4. Multiple questions are also helpful. This is where you ask two or more questions in one. Although this may sound confusing, the effect it has is quite interesting. The person replying hears multiple questions and usually interprets it as a request to tell you everything they know about a particular situation. It can be very successful in uncovering hidden information. Oddly, it is very rare that respondents answer the multiple questions clearly and succinctly in the order they were asked.

5. Leading questions are famously used by lawyers to get people to admit something they might not otherwise do. An example might

be, "Is it not true that you knew you would not be able to meet the delivery times when we placed the order?" Leading questions are often closed questions, as they request a one-word answer but rarely get one.

6. Reflective questions are helpful to calm a meeting down. It might be a way to summarize a situation. For example, "It seems to me that we are going to have to delay this project unless the equipment is delivered earlier." At first glance, this looks like a statement, but you are asking the other party to respond and either agree or explain why this isn't the case.

7. Finally, we have hypothetical questions. These are very useful tools for the negotiator. Also known as "what if" questions, these are good for exploring possibilities and suggesting possible trade-offs. For example, "What if we were able to give a two-year commitment; do you think you would be able to reduce your prices by ten percent?"

Table 9 below gives some good examples of good open questions and tips on listening skills.

Good Questions	Good Listening Skills
1. What can I do to help you?	1. Focus on the other person, and don't be distracted.
2. Can you explain the process?	2. Listen from their point of view.
3. How do you feel about it?	3. Work with their agenda, not yours.
4. Can you explain that further?	4. See the other person as a friend, not a threat.
5. What does everybody think?	5. Give them time to finish. Don't be afraid of silence.
6. What can we change to make this better?	6. Let their answers guide your questions.
7. What key results are we looking for?	7. Listen carefully to what they have to say.
8. What do we think went wrong?	8. Write notes to show you are paying attention.
9. What are the implications of this?	9. Be enthusiastic.
10. What has to be done?	10. Practice your active listening.

TABLE 9. GOOD QUESTIONING AND LISTENING

Always take a trusted colleague with you, so you can work together. It can be very difficult to formulate a question accurately at the same time that you are listening to the nuances of an answer. Having a partner allows each of you to think around the situation while the other is asking questions. Good questioning and listening skills are the keys to gaining a proper understanding of your customers' requirements and priorities— feel free to use them as often as you can.

3.4 INFLUENCING OUTCOMES

Decisions are often made not based on facts but on judgments, percep-
tions, and even prejudices. This isn't necessarily a problem. The point here
is that you need to understand the priorities of your peers and colleagues.
You need to understand the basis that they are using to make their decisions. When salesmen do their strategic sales analyses, they review all
of the key decision makers and look at their motivations and decision
criteria. IT managers need to do the same—understand the priorities of
each key decision maker. Specifically, when doing your evaluation, think
of the following:

1. What are the objectives of the other departments?

2. Who are the key players?

3. What are their motivations and behaviors?

4. What are the biggest influences they currently have? (In terms of
   people they know, projects they run, and so on).

Think carefully as to what the decision makers will gain personally from
a decision (for example, less work, less hassle, personal glory, and so on) and
what their department will gain from the decision (more revenue or profitability, a better way of working for staff, or improved customer satisfaction).
Then match your offering to the requirements of those decision makers.

Psychologists are generally in agreement that people are born differently. Everyone sees the world and makes decisions in different ways.
This might seem like an obvious statement, but it has important ramifica-
tions. When I was first introduced to the theory, I still held onto the belief
that everyone basically thought the way I do, and their outlook was only
slightly different because of their past experience. I thought that if they
radically disagreed with me, they were either stupid or just being awkward. Of course, this is fundamentally not the case!

This it is very important for technical people to understand. The personality type of 60 percent of IT managers is such that they will tend to see the detail in situations. They will make their decisions based on factual information. In contrast, 70 percent of CEOs do not see the detail in situations, unless it is clearly presented. They have a summary view of the world—not because they are doing a different job (although this has some influence), but because they see the world differently. Similarly, a high percentage of marketing directors will make decisions based not just on the facts but on intangible factors. These decisions, which are often instinctive, are a complete anathema to many IT people.

So, in short, present to your audience in their preferred style as shown in Table 7 below.

	Where you might find them	How to attract their attention	How to annoy them
Logical and Structured	Accountants, IT professionals, sales managers	Structured, accurate, to-the-point presentations. Clear logical basis for findings and support material, if required.	Lots of detail that isn't relevant. Mistakes, such as adding errors. Illogical statements. Woolly and unstructured thoughts.
High-Level Thinkers	CEOs, lawyers, sales managers	High-level presentation in what is called an inductive or "pyramid" style. Start at the top level with logical layers of detail below, if required. Logical business models. Start with the summary.	Detailed and drawn-out presentations. Too much information. Keeping slides back; showing one bullet at a time.
Creative	Marketing directors	Creative imagery, out-of-the-box thinking, clear vision.	Being ungracious and impatient. Too many facts and data.
Friendly	HR managers	One-on-one discussions talking about specific situations in the here and now. Showing consideration for individuals in the company.	Being ungracious and impatient. Getting down to business without first taking the time to build a relationship.

TABLE 10. CHOOSING THE RIGHT INFLUENCING STYLE

Our ability to build relationships and influence across our organization is at the heart of this. You need to adjust your approach according to the window that your audience looks through. For example, do not try to give lots of detail to a CEO, who sees the world in summary. Use pictures, impressions, and imagery to influence a typical marketing director.

FIVE RULES FOR PRESENTING IT TO SENIOR EXECUTIVES

1. Be strategic, with a clear message and presentation logic. Ask for what you want at the beginning. Your presentation may be cut short for any number of reasons.

2. Make any slide presentation short and sharp and the visuals clear and concise. During your preparation, keep asking yourself if something is relevant, and if it isn't, take it out. Too much detail makes it more likely you will get sidetracked. Check that your numbers are accurate and add up correctly.

3. Practice, practice, and then practice some more. You should be able to give your presentation without slides. Practicing is a great way to test whether your presentation has a clear thread. Ask a colleague to play the devil's advocate.

4. Let them learn what they should know or have forgotten. For example, if you are asking for $500,000 for an upgrade from version 7 to version 8 of the CCBS, you need to remind the audience what the CCBS is and how the business will benefit from the upgrade. Don't leave half the audience wondering if they should pluck up the courage to ask what it means (customer care and billing system as it happens).

5. Stay alert. Don't lecture, and don't start off brief and then go verbose. Aim to complete your presentation in half the allotted time, and use the rest of the time for questions. Most of your audience will have read ahead anyhow, so don't keep them waiting, and encourage them to express their views.

TABLE 11. FIVE RULES FOR PRESENTING TO SENIOR EXECUTIVES

3.5 GUIDING CONVERSATIONS

When we suggest something—for example, how we might implement a new project—we may find that our sponsors are not in agreement. They may have several objections to the ideas put forward. Typical objection-type questions might be:

- Why will it take so long?

- Why is this so expensive?

- How come my fourteen-year-old son can create a database in an afternoon, and yet it takes you more than two months and half a million dollars?

If you are programmed to react the wrong way, then you will. In other words, if you see objections as negative, then your answer will sound defensive. But they are perfectly reasonable questions, particularly if—as in the example above—the project is expensive and going to take quite a long time. These objections are, in fact, merely a request for more information. Far from being negative, objections are usually a positive sign and provide the perfect opportunity to address valid concerns. Sales executives will tell you that when a prospective customer has no objections or comments to a proposal, it usually means that they are not interested and won't buy.

So, to return to the example above, when the business sponsor asked the question about lead time, she may not have been aware that the user experts wouldn't be available for three weeks or that new functionality was added in at the last minute, requiring a completely different system configuration. So, what is the best way to approach objections? The following table gives our top seven tips for handling objections:

HANDLING OBJECTIONS

1. Try and handle them in advance—in other words, before the main meeting.

2. Take time to listen to the requirement. Don't argue or interrupt.

3. Think carefully about why this situation might be different for this client.

4. Keep discussing options (together).

5. Ask what other options they would consider or have considered.

6. Talk about how others clients have felt in similar situations and what they found.

7. Recognize an objection might just be a grouse. "Why will it take so long?" might just be a negotiation ploy to see if you can deliver it earlier, but it does not necessarily mean that you have to.

TABLE 12. TECHNIQUES FOR HANDLING OBJECTIONS

Let us assume that all the objections have been overcome in a mutually agreeable way. What happens next? Well, if you were a salesperson, you would instinctively ask for the order—what is known in sales parlance as "closing the sale." Salespeople are very interested in this because it is the stage before they receive their commission. It is where they get the *commitment* to go ahead with the order. Table 13 gives some examples of useful techniques for obtaining commitment from users and business sponsors.

Closing is a really valuable tool that every IT manager should master. It is the most effective way to get a commitment from your business sponsors and users. Closing techniques should be used to gain incrementally smaller commitments. As stated earlier, timing is everything, and the commitment requested has to be reasonably in line with the discussion. Step-by-step commitments lead naturally to the final agreement. If the IT manager doesn't do this, a lot of work can be done without the agreement of the user or sponsor. At any time, they can turn around and say, "This is not what we wanted."

TECHNIQUES FOR GAINING COMMITMENT

- **Be assumptive**—This is when you believe your business sponsor has made up her mind to go ahead. You can say something like, "Shall we draw up the business plan, then, and present it together at the capital committee meeting?"

- **"Sounds to me"**—This is where you say something like, "It sounds to me as though you are happy to go ahead and…"

- **Two alternatives**—This is one of the most common techniques used by salespeople. It gives the customer the choice between two options. "Do you want to go ahead with solution A or solution B?"

- **Standing room only**—"We need to close the books on this one, as our development resource is almost fully committed for the next three months with project Y."

- **Last chance**—This is telling your customer that you need to move ahead with this, as you understand the vendor is increasing its prices next month.

TABLE 13. TECHNIQUES FOR GAINING COMMITMENT

Think about using these closing guidelines in your meetings. Sometimes it is helpful to ask for a commitment, even when you know you won't get it. For example, you may be discussing the scope of a low-priority project that is drifting on. You might ask something like, "Would you be happy if we started work on a prototype for this?" fully expecting the reply, "Well, I don't think we are ready yet. My team is tied up with other things." Since this is what you suspected, you can now suggest, "Why don't we put it on hold then, for the time being?" knowing that it will probably never resurface. Clearly, it is better to focus your attention on what the customer really wants than to spread yourself across too many projects.

3.6 HIGH-LEVEL INFLUENCE

Having a good network of contacts is the best way to build political influence. Organizations are not democracies, and not everyone gets a chance to vote. Successful networkers choose their network opportunities carefully, recognizing that some managers carry more weight than others. Successful networking means that you will have the gravitas and executive support to influence important political decisions. Political decisions are by their nature difficult to predict. To the inexperienced manager, outcomes often appear to be illogical and sometimes unfair. So, rather than sulking that things aren't going as planned, it is much better to start the work on influencing to make things unfair in your favor. The following suggestions will help you build influence with other senior managers.

JANE'S STORY: "DO AS YOU ARE TOLD"

I had often noticed that some of my managers took up a lot more of my time than others. But I had never wondered what my boss thought of me from this point of view. I had heard, though, that good leaders can become difficult followers without realizing it.

For me, it started when I was given responsibility for a new group of project managers in Eastern Europe. They were scattered far and wide. I was stretched to the limit and kept taking up more of my boss's time in asking for advice. My boss was getting frustrated with me, because I asked her opinion and then argued against her suggestions. Looking back, I should have just said, "Good idea, Boss!"

Apparently, there comes a "tipping point" when employees earn a bad reputation. Once past this point, it becomes a self-fulfilling prophecy where they get blamed for everything. I suspect that I was approaching this point. Luckily, I averted disaster by recruiting someone to take over the project team but still report to me. It taught me the importance of being easy to manage—in other words, to keep a handle on when and how often I spoke to my boss and what we discussed. Now I think about the problem in advance, present a couple of options to talk through, and better listen to the advice I am asking for.

Don't Underestimate Them: Just because they don't know a lot about IT, don't assume they are stupid! They are clever enough to be more senior than you in the organization (for the time being, at least.) Always seek their opinion, even if you aren't sure that they have one. Be warned; some managers deliberately try to appear a bit slow. It is a tactic that often uncovers additional information.

Don't Ever Tell Them They Can't Do Something: It'll just make them cross, and they'll do it anyhow. An example comes to mind of a story told to me by Gloria, the head of customer care for a technology firm in Boston. She was told by the IT department that it wouldn't be possible to implement a new customer care scripting module. For her, this was not an option. It was vital that new customer care representatives could handle calls as soon as they joined. And the scripting system would provide this. So, she hired some programmers and did it herself. It was professionally done and highly effective. The IT department looked unresponsive as a result.

Don't Take Too Long in Your Conversations: Start with the punch line. Ask for what you want, and tell them what they will get in return and when. Don't expect to receive specific instructions. Senior executives are often too busy to work out the details; indeed, they may not have the expertise to do it. Often, explaining in outline what you plan to do is just what they want to hear. Once you have your agreement, don't hang around, just make it happen. Avoid coming back to them with too many questions, but do get back to them when it is finished.

Don't Expect Them to Be Warm and Cuddly: Don't take abuse personally; it is one of the unfortunate facts of our hectic, e-mail-centric lives that senior managers can often be very curt, which can, in turn, appear rude. Even so, treat all managers with respect. Be confident—it is important that you speak regularly to senior managers and feel comfortable in their presence. Hang onto your sense of humor, but don't necessarily force it on them. What may be amusing to you may not be to others.

Take Extra Care of Your Boss: Your boss is important to the business and important to you. You may or may not like your boss, but you need to be clear in understanding that he or she has enormous influence over you and your success. Your boss is essential though for you to succeed. Keep them fully informed of your actions, and make them aware of your achievements. Support your boss; even compliment them from time to time. Ask what is on their mind, and take an interest in their priorities.

Act with Integrity: The most important political lesson of all. Managers who deceive to get what they want will find that it comes back to haunt them. Better to take time and build relationships on a platform of trust. Identify key players in political decisions and put forward your arguments to them clearly, logically, and concisely.

3.7 POLITICS AND THE BALANCE OF POWER

Building good networks is about growing your influence, both inside and outside of your organization. As we have said before, it is about making life unfair in your favor. But this can sometimes be misconstrued as being devious. When we ask delegates what words come to mind when they think of company politics, we often get words like *manipulative, secretive*, and so on. But this is misleading. Politics can be very positive.

Politics is defined as the process by which groups of people make collective decisions. In practical terms, this is the art of making decisions, where not everyone has the same end goals in mind. Decisions are therefore made based on influence and power. Of course, by their nature, collective decisions and actions will not suit everyone. And hence, there can be a temptation for some parties to use underhanded methods to get what they want. Understanding these currents is essential to good political management.

In fact, there are two factors when it comes to politics. First of all, being effective at politics requires presence and influence, as we have already discussed. The second factor is how this influence or power is used. The first rule of corporate politics states that whoever has the most power, always wins—except it is not always obvious where the power lies. It is a complex combination of different factors as shown in Figure 6.

The Balance of Power—Who Will Win?

Positive Power	Negative Power
Seniority	Low-ranking position
Good links to key sponsors	Few links to key sponsors
A wide network of influence	Limited network of influence
Strong presence	Weak presence
Good track record	Indifferent track record
A plan for success	A list of complaints

FIGURE 6. THE BALANCE OF POWER

A technique we use on the IT leadership course for predicting political outcomes may help. It recognizes that political decisions are made in large part by consensus. And even though one person in the room may be more senior than the others, that person rarely makes the decision unilaterally. Indeed, it would be very unwise for such a manager to abuse their power and vote against the rest of the group on a regular basis. Sensibly, these people look to see what the overall view of the room is and periodically assess the balance of the decision. If their view coincides with the consensus view then there is no problem. They may take care if someone whose opinion they really value does not agree. And if there is no strong view, they will take the decision themselves. If they are experienced, they may also use what I call the "finishing line technique." If a decision is ebbing and flowing, they may wait until it flows the way they want and use their seniority to close the discussion (cross the finish line), thereby appearing to be abiding by the meeting consensus but actually using their influence to choose a preferred outcome.

The technique uses a rule of thumb to measure the balance of power of a decision; we take the "moment" of influence. This is the product of multiplying the strength of a person's view (positive of negative) with their weight of influence (as determined by the factors in Figure 6). So, to give an example, a highly influential person who is slightly opposed to an idea might be similar in the balance of power to someone who is strongly in favor but not quite so influential. This also helps in where to spend your influencing time. If you can move an influential person from being slightly opposed to being neutral or slightly in favor of your proposals, this can have a very positive impact on the outcome. Similarly, if you can invite someone to the room who supports you, that may help, and vice versa. Hopefully you get the idea. Suffice to say, a mathematical (or mechanical) view of political influence will only get you so far. If a decision needs so much political maneuvering, it may be worth letting this one go and focus one's energies on more obvious causes.

Let us not be naïve here. To be successful in managing your network and influence, you need to understand the political currents within your organization. There are many situations that generate strong internal political currents. Learn how to recognize them. Examples include managers under pressure and managers underperforming; company acquisitions and mergers; two departments at odds; corporate programs (projects); and budget and investment planning.

It helps to be streetwise when it comes to politics but not to play games. Game players invariably get found out and end up having to move on. The following suggestions might help.

Take Your Opportunities: Politically aware managers have an acute sense of timing. A decision that lands one way on one day, may land the other way on the next. As a technology manager, you will invariably have come across some examples of this, perhaps where the finance approval committee has held off on an infrastructure investment. So, in this case, a good time to resubmit a request might be shortly after the next outage. Just try to avoid looking smug.

CATHERINE'S STORY: WHAT HAPPENED THERE?

Someone was telling me about how teachers handle problems on the playground. If children (normally boys) are being a nuisance, experienced teachers will not tell them to stop it. Instead, they will try to join in, and they take the steam out of the situation that way. When I was told this, I was reminded of a situation at work. One department did not want to pursue a particular project. They assigned someone from their own department to join the project. Whether purposefully or not, this person subtly but persistently undermined the project by being helpful in an unhelpful way. In time, the project stalled. At the time, I thought nothing of it, but looking back, maybe things weren't as innocent as I had first imagined.

Avoid Bogus "Development Opportunities": Be wary if someone offers you a chance to work on a project that sounds too good to be true, offering great promises of career enhancement, gold bullion, and the like. Development opportunities, even difficult ones, are to be welcomed. But if you are being offered an opportunity where the previous incumbent was not successful, it is vital that you find out why and gain any necessary commitments in terms of budget, resources, and management support. In summary, do not accept new assignments blindly.

Don't Be Bullied: Coercing people is forcing them to make a decision that they might not otherwise make. An example might be right before an important meeting, where one manager threatens the interests of another unless he or she is supported. Another more subtle form is name dropping—mentioning the name of someone senior who supports you and suggesting this person will be unimpressed if the other person does not support you as well.

By way of conclusion, here is a summary of some other political dos and don'ts.

Some Political Dos and Don'ts	
Don't: • Ignore the balance of power. • Play against someone more powerful than you. • Think you are invincible. • Spend too much time in your own work group. • Focus only on immediate results. • Assume small players have no influence.	**Do:** • Cultivate players who can build your leverage. • Build your "page rank" around the company with more links. • Use your position as an IT manager at the heart of the business. • Be smart, and make things work in your favor. • Act with integrity.

TABLE 14. SOME POLITICAL DOS AND DON'TS

4. Technology Innovation

4.1 THE INNOVATION ROLE OF THE CIO

Innovation isn't about big ideas. It is about *new* ideas, doing things in different and better ways. Successful innovators know that small, medium, and large ideas are all vital to success. And no one else is better qualified than IT to lead the way. In the new digital age, CIOs must lead innovation. Although innovation should transcend the whole organization and is not just the responsibility of senior management, the CIO is uniquely placed to lead it. Innovation is everywhere, but rarely does it happen without technology. And we need lots of ideas to keep the fire burning. Ideas to do the following:

1. Support marketing, build new clients, and improve customer loyalty

2. Improve the working relationships with users, and make life easier for customers

3. Improve the processes embedded in applications, productivity, and working conditions

4. Make better information available in better ways for employees, customers, and shareholders

5. Use new technologies in ways that have not been thought of

Innovation is nothing new to IT managers. IT has for a long time had a pioneering culture and method for small, incremental type enhancements; we call it continual service improvement. And over twenty years ago, we were at the heart of large-scale IT innovation called business process reengineering—the radical redesign of processes, pioneered by Michael Hammer in the 1990s.

Very few real innovations in business happen without technology. And technology innovation is the responsibility of the CIO. There are many innovation leadership opportunities for the savvy IT professional to set up the framework for innovation, build innovation communities, provide wide-ranging sources of technology ideas, and drive the quest to do more and do it better.

Although the search for new ideas can be a source of inspiration, it can also provoke fear and anxiety. That should come as no surprise. At its heart, innovation is about finding something new, something new that, by its nature, does not exist today. Talk about stressful!

This excerpt from John F. Kennedy's speech about sending a man to the moon, delivered at Rice University in 1962, captures it for me:

"But if I were to say, my fellow citizens, that we shall send to the moon, 240,000 miles away from the control station in Houston, a giant rocket more than 300 feet tall, the length of this football field, made of new metal alloys, *some of which have not yet been invented*, capable of standing heat and stresses several times more than have ever been experienced, fitted together with a precision better than the finest watch, carrying all the equipment needed for propulsion, guidance, control, communications, food, and survival, on an untried mission, to an unknown celestial body, and then return it safely to Earth, reentering the atmosphere at speeds of over 25,000 miles per hour, causing heat about half that of the temperature of the sun and do all this, and do it right, and do it first before this decade is out—*then we must be bold*."

This makes two key points. First of all, the project was undertaken before they knew it could be done. And secondly, it required courage and leadership. It is our job as leaders to inspire our teams to take on the challenge and guide them through the challenge and uncertainty. To do this, we need a clear view of what the end vision will look like. We cannot afford for this to be vague and woolly; instead, we need to be ambitious and precise. And, we need to provide the lanterns that light the way.

4.2 A CULTURE OF INNOVATION

IT leaders need to educate everyone that innovation is everyone's responsibility and that everyone can do it. Ideas should be coming from everywhere e.g., the service desk, business analysts, project managers, operations specialists, not just a few energetic managers. Teaching and motivating staff on the importance of innovation can be done in many ways, but however it is done, it needs a coordinated effort. A good way to do this is with an innovation training program, reinforced on a regular basis. One client we worked with used Friday afternoons as their IT innovation window. The meeting was started with a quick reminder on the need for innovation and the behaviors necessary for generating and following through with good ideas.

When you consider the constant pressure and anxiety of searching for new ideas, it is no surprise that the IT leadership team needs to be regularly nudging people back into the innovative mindset. To sustain it, the leadership team needs to think about how to embed it within the departmental culture. The following guidelines should help:

Promoting a Culture of Innovation
1.   Appoint innovation pioneers—You won't have time to do it all yourself. Although people can be inspired to think differently, it is necessary to have someone guiding the process. Innovation pioneers form innovation teams with a combination of good technology knowledge, creative thinking, and strong leadership.
2.   Provide training—Help staff to understand the process of innovation, explain what innovative behaviors look like, and allay their anxieties and encourage creativity. A key part of innovation training is making sure that everyone understands that it is their responsibility.
3.   Give people unstructured time—3M and Google give their employees about 10 percent free time to work on personal (innovation) projects. Atlassian gives employees the chance to work on anything that relates to their products, and deliver it during ShipIt Day, their twenty-four-hour hackathon.
4.   Provide day-to-day leadership—Remind team members to always be looking to challenge the way things are done and asking, "Why do we do it this way?" and "Is there a better way?"
5.   Change the working environment—Examples include creating separate chill out areas, specially landscaped gardens and colorful and playful, creative meeting spaces. Once company has idea white boards around the office, and staff post problems they want help with, and team members add ideas.
6.   Encourage networking—Innovators spend a lot of time and energy finding and testing ideas through a diverse network of individuals. Retain top talent. Encourage networking outside immediate responsibilities. Develop "connectors" who can forge links across the business. Loosen formal controls, but tighten interpersonal connections between innovation efforts and the rest of the business.

TABLE 15. PROMOTING A CULTURE OF INNOVATION

Learning is a vital part of innovation. Three of the five attributes (questioning, observing, and experimenting) of the innovator's DNA are important sources of learning. The fourth (networking) is a priority for the IT leadership team and requires the building of wide and varied connections and sources of influence. The fifth (associative thinking) comes to the fore in the creation of new ideas using information gathered from the first three and is discussed with a diverse network of talented people.

Innovators like to ask questions. They ask a lot of why questions. Why do we do it this way? A low context (less hierarchical) society promotes a culture of innovation as it makes it easier for people to question. 5W + H (who, what, when, where, why, and how) is a common innovation technique used for gleaning more information about the problem. State the problem in the format "In what way might…we work more closely with the users?" Then write down a separate list of questions using who, what, when, where, why, and how. Separate each of the 5Ws and the H. Use these questions to generate a problem definition.

Innovators watch the world around them. They are often avid readers, taking an interest in topics not directly related to their own worlds. Think about what sources of information might help you to expand your outlook. IT and business journals are an obvious start. Perhaps there are relevant journals that report on innovations in your industry to give ideas on how your competition are solving problems. Choose your information carefully. A lot of time can be wasted reading long articles that are basically thinly disguised sales pitches.

IT professionals are good at learning. They take in information readily. But they can sometimes struggle with using that information and translating it into good ideas or getting into the creative mindset, as it were.

Part of the problem is that many people think that innovative thinking is genetic. That you are either born with it, or you're not. In fact, the opposite is true. The research suggests that creativity can be developed and that only 30 percent of our creativity performance can be attributed to genetics (whereas over 80 percent of general intelligence can be attributed to genetics.) To put it a different way, two thirds of our innovation skills come through learning. So, all the more reason to open ourselves up to new learning.

Science shows that we need to be relaxed for creative thought. This also explains why it is that we often have our best ideas when we are least expecting them. The BBC television show, *Horizon Special*, aired in 2013, and the team looked at innovation and spoke to Dr. Rex Jung, from the University of New Mexico. He had studied numerous brain scans as people let their minds wander and had noticed a distinct change in the frontal lobe of the brain. This part of the brain essentially provides our self-control. So, if we can relax our self-control, we can allow ideas from our subconscious to percolate through into our conscious awareness. Dr. Jung called this process hypofrontality. Different people induce this through different ways. Some like to mow the grass, some go for a jog, some use meditation. In our innovation sessions, we use a number of techniques, including simple mathematical games.

The creative mindset is different from the normal business way of thinking. It is more playful, more creative. It needs to generate new, exciting, and sometimes slightly crazy ideas. So, to some extent, it needs to be turned on and off. Serious governance, audit, or security meetings, for example, might not be the best place to jump up and shout, "Eureka!"

Experimenting is also an important component of innovation. Many famous entrepreneurs had several business failures before they ultimately achieved success. Thomas Edison is famously quoted as saying, "I have not failed. I've just found 10,000 ways that won't work," and "Many of life's failures are people who did not realize how close they were to success when they gave up." Experimentation can be trial and error, but in the world of IT, it is often evolutionary. It is common to find something that sort of works and then enhance it one step at a time. As an IT leader, if you want to encourage innovation, you also need to encourage experimentation. And this means providing budgets to allow it and being realistic about success rates.

4.3 THE PROCESS OF INNOVATION

Although innovation needs to be free flowing, it also needs some boundaries to be effective. Innovation should not be confused with blue sky thinking or invention. "Most innovations, especially the successful ones, result from a conscious purposeful search for innovation opportunities."[24] To get the most value out of innovation, it needs to be guided. The process should be light and appropriate. It needs to encourage innovation at every level but still allow business to run in the meantime.

The diagram below gives an example of how innovation can work. It starts in the top right-hand corner with strategy and culture. If the board of directors sets strategic objectives that rely on innovation, it must also put in place the organizational culture to deliver it. With a foundation of strategy and culture, the business can get on with the business of innovating.

For innovation to thrive, it needs everyone to ask questions and set problems to solve. These questions can come from high-level objectives (How can we increase revenue in product line *x*? or improve system reliability in data center *y*?) or day-to-day problems (How can we get this project back on track? or How can we image new laptops more efficiently, improve user training, reduce performance bottlenecks, or improve quality of customer data?) An innovation culture encourages everyone to ask questions everywhere and always.

---

24 Peter Drucker, "The Discipline of Innovation," *Harvard Business Review*, August 2002.

The process of innovation

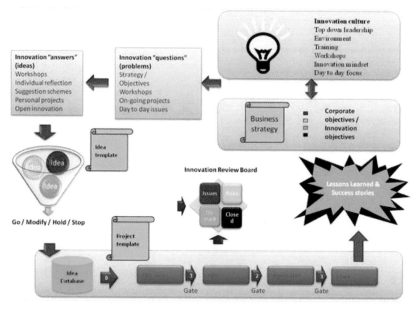

FIGURE 7. THE PROCESS OF INNOVATION

To get the most out of our process, every innovation question asked should generate a range of possible ideas to solve it. And so, the more opportunities for generating ideas the better. The process diagram above suggests workshops, individual reflection, open innovation, and suggestion schemes as possible sources. Some will be worked on as soon as they are asked (e.g., in innovation workshops); some will held open for a longer period (open innovation). Experience from innovation workshops tells us that in general, innovation questions are at least as important as generating innovation answers (ideas).

For innovation to perpetuate, there needs to be a visible process for assessing ideas and putting them into practice. An innovation review board, staffed by the right people, is the most common way to do this. The board reviews ideas and either approves them, suggests modifications, puts them on hold, perhaps for a more suitable time, or rejects them. When a project is approved, the board needs to give guidance on what is expected. It needs to be realistic about results and assign the appropriate amount of budget and resource. It is potentially at this point that the group can talk about how much experimentation is allowed. Innovation projects can be measured with a standard project pipeline methodology. Closedown reports are done in the same way, with outcomes fed back to the innovation board and the strategy. So, let us look at the elements in a bit more detail.

In its simplest form, IT is there to provide technology solutions to business problems. The application of new technology to solve these problems is technology innovation. The process we describe above is quite simple. Find some problems to solve and use innovation techniques to solve them. IT departments can offer another innovation path: "We'll tell you what technology solutions exist and help you find problems they might solve." I call this two-way approach "hammers and nails." You can start with a hammer (the technology) and look for a nail to hit (the business problem), or you can be given a nail and then go find the right hammer. Both are equally valid, but a word of caution with the first one. Sometimes, when all you have is a hammer, everything looks like a nail! Many CIOs have rued their swift forays into outsourcing or cloud solutions before the business case was sufficiently robust and the technology proven. In other words, just because a technology can offer great potential benefits to the world in general, it does not necessarily mean it will to your own organization.

4.4 FINDING PROBLEMS TO INNOVATE

To simplify our process for fostering innovation, we can focus on three simple steps:

FIGURE 8 - THE HEART OF THE INNOVATION PROCESS

Problems and objectives are kind of similar when we talk about innovation. There may be a "problem" that calls are taking too long to answer. This may equally manifest itself as "We would like to answer calls more quickly," or "Our objective is to handle calls ten seconds faster." Problems will be defined in many different ways.

Setting objectives around problems that we encounter is an important component of the innovative organization. We all have our annual business or IT objectives that we focus on during the year. If possible, think about setting innovation objectives. These are a bit like the John F. Kennedy objectives about sending a man to the moon. When setting these objectives, you will, by definition, not yet know how (or indeed if) they will be realized. Infosys, the Indian offshore company, asks all of its senior executives to include two innovation objectives alongside their regular business objectives. Innovation objectives are, by definition, stretch objectives.

Problems ripe for innovative thinking come up all the time, without us necessarily asking for them. As if you hadn't enough on your plate, here are some techniques to generate additional ones I have used in workshops.

We call the first technique "ladder of excellence." Let us suppose that we are having problems with our new starter process. The idea is to list all the characteristics of the process on a scale from one to ten. Those characteristics that are handled very well are rated higher and listed higher on the chart. Those handled less well are obviously near the bottom. The benefit of the scale is that rational discussions can take place as to why each characteristic is where it is. You can put up and down arrows, representing forces with labels. An up arrow would have a label referring to a positive aspect. A down arrow would represent a negative attribute or problem.

PATRICK'S STORY: NOT ENOUGH PROBLEMS?

I had been asked to facilitate a workshop for a government organization based in Washington DC. The IT department had been set up as a joint venture with a leading IT systems integrator. The government organization had set up a client function facing off to the IT joint venture. Their responsibility was to ensure that high quality, robust systems were delivered to address priorities, on time, and in budget. The IT team were worried that the delivery of systems was technically good, but that the client was unhappy. They had no specific evidence that this was the case, but had brought me in to bring the sides closer together.

My brief was to run the innovation workshop, encourage the client team to open up as to what was working and what could be done better, with a view to brainstorming innovative (or indeed simple) solutions to improve the situation. I followed the normal agenda, but because time was short, we perhaps spent less time warming up and not a whole lot of time identifying the problems. What few problems we discussed were solved. But we were left feeling that not everything was out in the open.

Looking back, we had one shot at this, and since the client did not really have enough time, we should have postponed the meeting. By not giving them time to open up to us and discuss problems, we jumped too quickly to solutioning and missed our opportunity.

The second stage is to translate the ladder into problem statements. Look for those characteristics lower down the scale, and assess the negative attributes. One example I have encountered in the new starter process was the ordering of new laptops for new starters. A positive aspect was that the laptops were brand new. Negative aspects included that they weren't there on day one and didn't have the base applications installed. So, in terms of problems to solve, one is around immediate availability, and one is about having the right software installed.

Having positive and negative forces on the diagram helps people being too sensitive about identifying problems. It is also important that solutions to the problems are not worked on straight away. Having a good stock of problems to solve is vital for the process to work. And if people get distracted and go straight into solution mode, the momentum is usually lost.

Notes on Effective Innovation Workshops
Although problems will come from anywhere and everywhere, innovation efforts very often come from focused workshops. Much of our work on innovation is facilitating workshops. We have learned some important things to get people in the right mindset.
1. Set some ground rules for the meeting. These include no criticism or analysis during idea generation. All ideas should be welcomed. Freewheeling must be encouraged to identify as many ideas as possible. Recognize that everybody has different viewpoints, and they should be treated with respect.
2. Give the background of the innovation meeting. Are there any particular problems that need attention? How much time is available? Does the meeting need to find the answer today? It is also helpful to explain the process being used.
3. Give some examples where it has worked before. *How to Have Kick-Ass Ideas* by Chris Barez-Brown[25] has some great examples of innovation in practice. Remind people of the quote by Charles Swindoll, "We are all faced with a series of great opportunities brilliantly disguised as impossible situations."
4. Play some games. This can be particularly helpful when the group members do not know each other particularly well. As an aside, the science also says that the best ideas come when the innovation meeting comprises members of loosely connected groups.

TABLE 16. EFFECTIVE INNOVATION WORKSHOPS

The second technique is a simple brain-storming technique that can also be used for idea generation. Participants write down problems on Post-it® notes. After about ten to fifteen minutes, each group reclaims their own Post-it® notes and sticks them on the wall, reading out or explaining the statement. At the end of the exercise, the problems are reviewed. Similar problems are grouped together. The problem sets can be processed in a couple of ways. If there is little correlation between the

---

25 Chris Barez-Brown, *How to Have Kick-Ass Ideas,* Skyhorse Publishing, 2008.

problems, the Post-it® can be put on a ladder of severity. Large problems are posted on the top half and smaller problems near the bottom. Alternatively, if there is correlation, they can be arranged in clusters, each cluster relating to a higher level problem. Decide on which ones you are going to address (it could be all of them.) Once you have done this, put together a clear problem statement that says which problem(s) is to be solved and any boundaries that may need to be put around it (them).

Scenario planning can also help here in starting the process of creative innovation. Set two or three different objectives around the same problem. So, we discussed earlier an example of reducing call answer time. For this, we might define two problem statements. The first scenario might be "How could we reduce it from thirty seconds to twenty seconds?" The second scenario might be "How could we reduce it from thirty seconds to less than five?" These different problem statements will require different techniques to generate ideas, described in the next section.

4.5 TECHNIQUES FOR GENERATING IDEAS

Many idea generation techniques have been invented to encourage new ideas. The list below includes those we find most useful. Again, most of them are designed for innovation workshops but work just as well in team meetings or even one-to-ones. I think experience has taught me that some of the more far-fetched techniques can be a bit counter-productive for IT teams. Fundamentally, IT people have a serious job of work to do and find it difficult to suddenly change into some wacky, child-like persona to come up with new ideas. The more time one has in a workshop, the more experimental you can be. That still doesn't alter the fact that lots of very good ideas come from simple methods. Different techniques will tend to generate more radical solutions. The techniques described below are roughly in order to generate increasingly radical ideas.

Brainstorming—The facilitator writes ideas on the flipchart, as they are suggested by the participants. Brainstorming was originally developed by Alex Osborn at BBDO and is the quickest and simplest method for identifying ideas. It has a couple of drawbacks, though. First of all, without

realizing it, the scribe at the front will often write down something a bit different from what was said. Secondly, those with the louder voices will tend to be the ones whose ideas are heard and written down.

Brain Writing (similar to brainstorming but overcoming the problems above)—Fold a few sheets of paper into small note-sized squares. Participants then write an idea on the note and put it in a central pool. When an individual needs stimulation, they can exchange their sheet of paper to spark different chains of thought and create new ideas. The ideas are then displayed on the wall, where they are explained and discussed further. I am a great believer in what I call secondary ideas. These are ideas that springboard from an original idea. This technique is brilliant for allowing this type of thinking.

Reverse Logic—Write down the problem statement, and reverse it in any way possible. Using the reversed definition, encourage participants to develop innovative ideas. One example might be, how to design the worst project process possible. From the list of "hilarious" ideas, you can then reverse the suggestion into something more positive. This technique is actually quite effective and can also be a very useful icebreaker. Unfortunately, some of the so-called negative suggestions will be things they are doing. If you have included your business stakeholders in the meeting, they will generally not be shy in listing a whole bunch of them.

Morphological Analysis—The fifth key skill of the innovator suggested in the paper "The Innovator's DNA" is that of associative thinking. This is the art of combining ideas from different areas, different experiences, different industries, different networks, and so on to create a new idea. Morphological analysis is a good technique for illustrating this. Participants break down problems or issues into smaller elements. List all the major elements involved in the issue or problem, and write them across the top of a flipchart or white board. Each sub-element is then listed under each element, and the facilitator asks the participants to start combining the separate elements together to try to ascertain some novel ideas. This is repeated until a sufficient number of ideas have been generated.

Pugh Matrix—The Pugh matrix develops this further. It is helpful in combining ideas from different possible solutions. It works well when there are three or four possible technical solutions for solving a particular problem. It combines different ideas and solutions to create a better one. It is designed to develop a win-win situation. On a large sheet of paper, list all the options that are being considered down the left-hand side. Across the top of the paper, list the main criteria being used to measure the options. Ask the participants to look at each criterion and list all the positive and negative aspects of each. Some options will have more positive aspects than negative aspects. Develop a new option that incorporates all or some of the positive aspects of the previous options, and relinquishes all the negative aspects.

Heuristic Ideation—Ask the group for a small list of random objects (three to five). Next, take one of your problem statements. Use each object to start a thought train as to how it, or something related to it, might solve the problem described in the problem statement. A generic problem we use on our courses is how to improve airports. The list of random objects might, for example, include flowers, Monopoly, and dogs. The idea is then to use these objects to set off trains of thoughts to develop new ideas. e.g., with flowers, one idea was to create a garden within the airport; Monopoly started a train of thought about setting up areas with some simple family friendly games. The *Creative Whack Pack*, a set of idea cards by Roger von Oech,[26] provides a great catalyst for generating new trains of thought.

Assumption Reversal—Write down the problem statement, and list all the assumptions that can be made regarding the problem or situation. Reverse each of the assumptions. Don't worry if they seem to be odd or ridiculous. Use these assumption reversals to stimulate new ideas regarding the problem or situation. For example, a computer requires electricity to operate might lead to the possible idea of building a solar-powered (or clockwork) computer.

---

26 Roger von Oech, *Creative Whack Pack,* US Games, 1992—a set of creative ideas on cards.

Business Process Reengineering—Reengineering is the fundamental rethinking and radical design of business processes to achieve dramatic improvements in critical contemporary measures of performance, such as cost quality service and speed. *Reengineering the Corporation*, by Michael Hammer and James Champy,[27] is an updated version of the original pioneering text on the subject. The new version looks also at the revenue producing side of the business and at ways to break down the walls that separate corporations from each other. One example I still recall from having the book some years ago came from IBM Credit. The old process had been overdesigned to handle the most difficult applications that management could envisage. Two senior managers had a brainstorm; they took a financing request and walked it through all five steps, asking personnel in each office to put aside whatever they were doing and process the request as they would normally. The actual work took ninety minutes instead of one to two weeks. Allowing the same person to perform different steps in a process is a typical outcome of reengineering. The roles tend to require more skill, but work is performed much more efficiently, and job satisfaction increases.

Wildest Idea—This technique is quite a radical one and is best done when the group is warmed up and relaxed. The facilitator asks the group participants to develop wild ideas about a particular situation. For example on parking solutions, a wild idea could be to knock down the office building and use the land for a giant parking lot, instead. Using a wild idea as a starting point, the participants can continue to generate ideas. This step is repeated until all the wild ideas have been used or until there are sufficient practical solutions that have been developed.

Paper Folding—This is a fun exercise that can also be done at the beginning of a workshop as a warm-up. It starts with a radical idea and then progresses it toward something more realistic. Each person starts with a blank piece of paper, writes something, and passes it on to the next person at each of the following stages:

---

27 Michael Hammer and James Champy. *Reengineering the Corporation*. Nicholas Brealey Publishing, 2001.

1. First, on the blank piece of paper, each person writes down a problem they wish to be solved

2. Then, the next person has to create a crazy, out of-the-box idea for solving it

3. Next, a crazy and unlikely solution but still scientifically possible

4. Then, a more practical solution to the problem

5. Finally, a second practical solution to the problem (either related or not)

Wishful Thinking—This is similar to role-play, but role-play is encouraged to be more radical, even unrealistic in the ideas. It is not the intention that the idea is put into practice but fuels the discussion to how close one might get. The group members are asked to write a brief statement of the problem. The facilitator tells the group to assume that everything is possible. Each individual then needs to develop some fantasy statements about the future using terms such as "In the future, it would be nice if the organization did…" Group members examine each fantasy statement and develop ideas on how these can be achieved.

4.6 FROM IDEAS TO IMPLEMENTATION

For any innovation session to be worthwhile, it is important that ideas are assessed and any valuable ones are taken forward and acted on. For many teams, this is often the most difficult part. It is difficult to compare ideas from completely different areas. Sometimes emotions run high, and it is helpful to have some techniques. Two in particular spring to mind. The first is the voting dots method. Each participant is given a fixed number of votes they can attribute to any of the ideas on the list. The ideas with the most dots or votes are chosen.

The second method derives from Edward de Bono's *Six Thinking Hats* method.[28] Edward de Bono is a pioneering author, inventor, and consultant. He originated the term "lateral thinking." He also recognized that a lot of innovation energy is wasted when people are not thinking in the same way. His *Six Thinking Hats* used the metaphor of a hat to symbolize particular thinking styles. In his book, Edward de Bono suggests a range of ways to use this. For myself, I like to use the hats in a sequence, with everyone adopting the same style at the same time. In outline, there are six hats, and I have listed them in the sequence that works well in innovation workshops:

1. Blue hat—This provides the cool thinking. It is good for getting people to think about what needs to be done. I use it as the stage for setting objectives or identifying the problems in general.

2. White hat—This is where you look at the facts of the problem. This is helpful for identifying the specifics of the problem. So, if the objective was to improve the poor image of IT on the helpdesk, the white hat would examine what exactly is wrong with the helpdesk.

3. Green hat—This is where (green and fertile) ideas are generated. The green hat is for constructive thinking.

4. Yellow hat—This is looking at ideas "sunny-side up." In other words, what are the positive aspects of the ideas being suggested?

5. Black hat—This is the black, devil's advocate, looking at the dark side of ideas. It will identify potential errors, risks, and dangers.

6. Red hat—Red for emotion, like a Ferrari! When participants are wearing the metaphorical red hats, they have the chance to express how they feel about an idea.

Getting IT people to think in the same way at the same time is very powerful and overcomes some typical problems that I encounter with IT

---

28 Edward de Bono. *Six Thinking Hats*. Penguin, 2009.

teams. The first is that they love to jump straight to "solution mode." Having the hat metaphor encourages the team to identify a broader range of problems and objectives before starting to find answers. Secondly, participants who have a dark and pessimistic outlook can quickly suck out the energy of the room and stifle creative energy. As soon as an idea is suggested, they can think of ten reasons why it will not work. Six hat thinking makes it more difficult for them to do this. But if they persist, organize the next one for when they are on vacation!

Yellow and black hat thinking is ideal for the rational evaluation of ideas, looking at the upsides (yellow hat) and downsides (black hat). The red hat recognizes that for all the logic and rationale in an idea, people still need to express an opinion. Fortunately, if you look at the plus and minus sides first, you tend to get a much more measured opinion. This structured thinking prevents the team from debating the merits of every idea at random and helps to reduce the disagreements that might give rise to conflict and inaccuracy in selection.

Grouping ideas is an important step in bringing ideas to fruition. Mind mapping, a technique developed by Tony Buzan,[29] can help bring structure and clarity to the creative part of the workshop by linking problems with solutions with radial, logical connections. Pictures, colors, images, and symbols can also be added to bring ideas to life. Mind mapping helps to avoid the linearity of thought and enables radiant thinking and its subsequent associations.

Many innovation initiatives die on the vine. Good ideas generated in workshops stay there. The effort people needed to find time to attend the meeting in the first place has caused a backlog of other work, and ideas get left behind. One of the solutions is to properly divide up the agenda and time for the workshop. The following breakdown is typical:

1. 20 percent for getting people in the right mindset

---

29 Tony Buzan, *The Mind Map Book: Unlock Your Creativity, Boost Your Memory, Change Your Life*, BBC Active, 2009.

2. 25 percent for defining the problems

3. 30 percent for creating ideas

4. 15 percent for grouping and ranking ideas

5. 10 percent for next steps and actions

Time keeping is important. If problem definition or idea creation over-runs, lots of ideas get generated, but no actions result.

Typically, ideas that come out of the innovation workshop are put forward to the Innovation Board. Innovations need to be presented in the right way. A little bit of pre-thinking can significantly help the board decide to progress an idea. Thought should be given as to how much experimentation might be required for the idea to be properly shaped. And, how much experimentation is allowed before the group concludes that the idea is not going to work out. Don't push a bad idea too far because it restricts the time of working on good ideas.

A stage-gate process is therefore helpful for progressing ideas through to fruition. Feeding back interim status reports to the innovation board will help them to reassess the viability of an idea, potentially change the focus of experimentation and/or development, and assign additional budget, if appropriate. Although innovation boards can give the impression of slowing down creativity, it is important the innovation teams stay focused and understand that this is not an academic exercise. Finally, when ideas are successful, it is important that proper rewards are given. It is the job of the CIO to promote good innovation work and highlight successes.

4.7 MEASURING IT INNOVATION

So, how do we measure innovation in IT. This is an interesting question. I was fortunate to work with Pernod Ricard, an international drinks company, facilitating their CIO conference. They had just received a high accolade as one of the top innovating companies in the world, as measured by the Forbes Innovation Premium.

The Innovation Premium metric was created by Jeff Dyer and Hal Gregerson. It is calculated first by projecting a company's income (cash flows, in this case) from existing businesses, plus anticipated growth from those businesses, and look at the net present value (NPV) of those cash flows. The net present value of cash flows from a business is then compared with its market capitalization.

Companies with a current market cap above the NPV of cash flows have an innovation premium built into their stock. In simple terms, this means that the stock market is expecting the company to generate revenues that cannot be foreseen from existing products and markets. In other words, they have put their faith in the company innovating. It could be argued that there are other factors that might give a high Innovation Premium score, however, history suggests that innovation is the strongest contributor. A more detailed explanation is given in *The Innovators DNA* (Harvard Business Press, 2011), written with Harvard Business School professor Clayton Christensen.

So, how does this translate to an IT department? The IT department does not have a stock price or market capitalization. You might argue that the continuous reduction in budgets is just the finance department's way of showing how much faith they have that IT will continue to do better year after year. The most practical way to measure IT's innovation index may be to look at the business case predictions (an explanation of cash flows, net present value, and returns on investment is given in *Excellent IT Management*).

Predicted innovation value = $\sum$ (all net present values from approved innovation projects)
Actual innovation value = $\sum$ (delivered net present values from approved innovation projects).

The more you invest in innovation, the higher you would expect the NPV to be, but the relative returns might diminish to unacceptable levels. In this case, it may make sense to cumulate all the business cases in IT and generate an overall Internal Rate of Return. This allows you to compare the return of innovation investment year after year. It also requires that projects be divided into "innovation projects" and "business as usual projects." How a company differentiates between these two will vary. One way to do it might be to say a business as usual project is one that adds capacity to existing business systems. Innovation projects would then be those that add new capability (new systems, new features, improved processes, etc.).

There is a complication here. IT departments, IT conferences, the IT press, and every other facet of the world of IT has been hung up with measuring IT value. The truth is there are many competing factors. If you measure the actual benefits realized from the IT projects, it will almost certainly come to a different number from the one predicted in the business case (usually a lower one!). On top of this, how many of the benefits delivered by a new project were just down to the technology? And how much down to improved productivity in the department? How many were down new products being launched at the same time? It is impossible to get an accurate number on this breakdown because of the subjectivity. It should, though, be possible to measure the overall advantage in a way not too dissimilar to the innovation premium index described earlier. The assumption is that from one year to the next, you can calculate the total value improvement in the business where IT innovation projects were a part. Assuming the breakdown as to what really delivered the benefit (systems, people, new products, etc.) stays roughly the same year after year, you get a useful metric.

4.8 LANTERNS TO THE FUTURE

All top IT executives keep up to date with the trends in technology, either through reading journals, attending conferences, or by talking to colleagues and their technology partners. When we poll delegates on our courses, however, we find that there is a gap between understanding the technology and converting it to business advantage. Every IT executive must have their own opinions on where technology is taking their business. They need to see into the future. But the future is not just one random moment in time. It never arrives. It is necessary to have a view for all points into the future. You need to know where the future will take you next year, the year after, and ten years after that. In your mind, you need to have a "time lapse" picture, showing how new technologies and innovations will build up, step by step, and how they will impact your business, your customers, and the competition. The final picture in your mind, the end point, that is your future vision. Don't just think about the arrival point because it never comes. Think about the individual technology steps that are implemented along the way; they are your lanterns to the future.

The following exercise might help you draw out how your business might evolve through the adoption of technology innovation. Use the blank diagram opposite to collate your ideas. Start with those technologies and projects that have recently been implemented. Then list those that are currently "in flight" for your organization. Thirdly, think about those technologies and trends that might be useful in the short or near term (say the next twelve months). Finally, think about those technologies that might be appropriate in the longer term.

	Recently implemented	In flight (projects already started & expected to deliver benefits in next year)	Available now (for implementation in next year or two)	Available now or expected in the next 1 to 2 years for implementation within 5 years
Projects / technologies				
Benefits				
Expected impact / change to culture & behaviours				
Other aspects				

FIGURE 9. ROADMAP FOR TECHNOLOGY AND INNOVATION

The exercise works best if you first put together a long list of possible technologies on a separate piece of paper. Filter the list to include those that are the most relevant. For example, three-dimensional printing—think about how it might be used by your organization in the future. You may conclude that there is no obvious or immediate benefit. Even so, it will help you to create your roadmap. Having an opinion as to why something is unlikely to be a major technology for you is as important as identifying those that will.

The intent here is to think about the flow of projects and technology change that will impact your business over the next ten years and in particular how it will change the day-to-day work. From a list of possible technologies, extrapolate the change impact for your organization, your competition, and the marketplace. Tracking through the changes builds up this "time lapse" picture of your business and industry. At the end, take a step back, and ask if this is plausible. What other scenarios might play out? The intent of the exercise is to strengthen *your opinion* on how your industry will change. Think about which technologies need more investigation. Talk to colleagues and technology partners to verify if they support your thinking. Are there any technologies or changes in working practices that should be brought forward to the senior executive? Having a clear and rational opinion of the technology future is the hallmark of a great IT leader.

4.9 SOME EXAMPLES OF INNOVATION

The following innovations have been chosen because they illustrate the different sources that innovation can come from.

An international law firm—This innovation was initiated by the IT department that was looking to promote mobility in the organization and was looking for opportunities to develop skills in writing mobile phone apps. They thought of possible ideas and decided to prototype an app that allowed the law firm partners to log their time from their mobile phones. This allowed them to capture time that had previously been unbooked because it was difficult to measure it retrospectively. The app was very well received by the lawyers, and apart from allowing significant additional time to be booked, provided a real enhancement to the image of the IT department.

British Transport—British Transport Police (BTP), recently won an innovation award for showing how technology, social media, and an informative online presence can improve passenger security. "Operation Magnum" was made up of a series of online videos that highlighted to passengers the thirteen most common methods of theft on public transport. Awareness of the threat of theft was also supported by the BTP twitter profile and the hashtag #EveryTheft. BTP also encouraged passengers to install tracker applications on their tablets and smart phones. The power of tracking technology in the professional hands of transport police is huge. There have been occasions of officers being able to trace a stolen phone from London all the way to Manchester and arrest the thief as he stepped onto the platform. BTP have a track record of innovation, pioneering the provision of vital information for police on mobile devices.

WSP Global—IT architect Paul Taylor gives a great example of the hammers and nails idea of innovation—in other words, the idea that you take a technology to the business and find problems it can solve. For them, it was the deployment of Microsoft Lync for presence, instant messaging, voice and video calling, conferencing, and desktop sharing. The business never asked for a solution to a problem; they had no idea what it was. WSP had signed a new Microsoft Enterprise Agreement, which included the Lync client licenses and were keen to get the most from them. Without the EA, it would probably have been difficult to get a buy-in for the specific costs of deploying Lync globally. It's not easy to "sell" something that people don't know they need. Two years later and Lync has changed the way the business works and collaborates to the point where most people's daily routine in the morning is plugging their headset in, ready for the day ahead.

First companies to off-shore—It was a trend that started many years ago, but special mention should be given to the first companies who off-shored services to India. The situation was that highly talented computer specialists were available for a fraction of the price being paid in the West, but differences in culture and time zones meant that there were serious practical risks. Those that innovated early got the best talent and the best prices. The barriers are eroding to some extent now, and even though other regions, such as Vietnam and Eastern Europe are competing in this space, it is the brave innovators and early adopters who gained the most.

My first experience with off-shoring was some time ago, and the process we followed was very much an innovation process and demonstrated that innovation applies to services as well as technology or products. We started with some less critical applications that were proving troublesome to maintain. The off-shore team did a superb job of fixing problems and then recommending possible enhancements. Because the price point was so low, we could afford to experiment and include additional opportunities that had not previously been considered. We thought a lot about the risks in the venture and put plans in place to mitigate them. Experimentation is important but should not be undertaken without consideration of the risks, and more importantly, the risks addressed.

Kanban boards—This is an interesting innovation in that it moved the organization away from the computer system. The Kaisen process and Lean IT that uses the principles of Kaisen (continual improvement) recognizes that computer systems are not always the answer. One IT manager was struggling to keep track on his management team that was working out of different offices in Europe. It wasn't particularly that he wanted to micromanage them but more that he could not get a hold of them when he needed them. It was possible to look at their calendars individually but was a cumbersome process.

The solution was to ask them on the Monday morning managers meeting to tell him what they were doing or e-mail it. He wrote these on a white board in his office, thereby creating what the Japanese would call a "Kanban" (which means signboard or billboard). The point is that for some applications the information needs to be immediately visible, not locked in a computer. This technique has been used in hospitals, where patient records were taken out of the computers and put back onto charts at the bottom of the patient's bed. This meant that the consultant visits were much more efficient, and problems with diagnosis or dosage could be easily spotted.

Virgin Airlines—Although not an IT example, the story Richard Branson tells about how he set up Virgin Atlantic is fascinating and insightful. He was trying to catch a flight to Puerto Rico with Joan, his fiancée; the local Puerto Rican-scheduled flight had been cancelled, and the airport terminal was full of stranded passengers. He made a few calls to charter companies and chartered a plane for $2000 to Puerto Rico (it was a long time ago!) He divided the price by the remaining number of passengers, borrowed a blackboard, and wrote: *VIRGIN AIRWAYS: $39 for a single flight to Puerto Rico*. He soon filled every seat on the plane. As they landed in Puerto Rico, a passenger turned to him and said, "Virgin Airways isn't too bad. Smarten up the services a little, and it could be in business." They have certainly done that. This is a fantastic example of innovating by opportunity.

RSPCA: (The Royal Society for the Prevention of Cruelty to Animals) demonstrates how developing a culture of innovation can yield benefits in many different areas. In the first instance, they demonstrated how a technology, in this case Google Drive, can be taken to business users as a potential solution to many different problems. Recent examples include using the Forms functionality within Google Drive, to create and deploy a number of secure online questionnaires and surveys. Google forms also collates real-time data from candidates and has been used to arrange major events and invitation logistics. It also recently supported a campaign on rabbit welfare.

The second source of innovation was where the business managers had a particular problem to solve. In this case, RSPCA signed a major agreement with Pets at Home whereby the RSPCA would have rehoming centres based in their shops. This means RSPCA cats were in pets at home stores, and IT used their innovation talents to develop a simple way to stream the cats in the centres to the website to a service called scratching post. This was a combination of a Raspberry Pi device, a webcam and a YouTube online stream. Brilliant, cheap and innovative. And in another innovation, the RSPCA created a virtual tour using Google's Street view cameras to allow web visitors to tour the rehoming sections, treatment rooms and so on.

5. Corporate Leadership

5.1 THE NEW ROLE OF THE CIO

CORPORATE LEADERSHIP IS THE SKILL SET REQUIRED BY THE CIO WORKING AT THE HIGHEST LEVEL IN AN ORGANIZATION. IT IS ABOUT the CIO influencing and changing the thinking of the top-level executive, molding its business strategy in line with the technology capability that the organization currently has and could have in the future. Corporate leadership is the transition the CIO makes, when he or she starts to guide the business, rather than being told what to do. Key roles for the corporate IT leader are:

1. A player in the business, no longer a spectator; the corporate IT is fully involved with key top-level issues, guiding the organization in all areas

2. The leader of IT governance, aligning IT results with the priorities of the business

3. The champion of IT's perception, promoting the culture of professionalism, responsiveness, and easy-to-use systems

4. The guardian of process integration, data integrity, and system security, making sure business stakeholders do not unilaterally take on solutions that damage end-to-end process integrity

5. Creator of a world-class IT organization

Much has been written over the years about the role of the CIO. My colleague, Dr. Robina Chatham, did some research a few years ago on the changing role of the CIO. The argument still goes on, and here is my chance to say a few things! First of all, the role of the CIO is not going away! Those who do not look after the new priorities and welfare of the business may disappear. CIOs are seated firmly at the center of an organization and see everything. They have a better view of the overall end-to-end functioning of the business than anyone else, including the CEO. All the interactions between departments, all the handoffs between processes, all data transactions are firmly in the line of sight of the CIO. When it comes to integrating the processes of the organization, the CIO is the orchestra leader.

The CIO is also a pioneer of innovation. Few innovations happen without technology innovation, either directly, as in the creation of a new technology product, or indirectly, as in the creation of software applications to enable to sale and delivery of new products. The CIO as the keeper of the technology world knows more than anyone about this. Other board members may have interactions with technology—the chief marketing officer with the company's digital online presence and the CFO with the ERP systems integration. But no one except the CIO has the end-to-end view.

Things are not quite as simple as they seem. Even though the role of the CIO is as important as ever, it does require some new skills. In the days of mainframes, the IT department was the only game in town. Systems, particularly for large organizations, were written in house. The IT department could be quite autocratic and arrogant (and usually was), insisting on particular solutions because they met the often arbitrary standards of the department. Things progressed with off-the-shelf systems, but IT still had to be involved to install the software because they had the keys of the data center. But then things moved on again. A bit like the privatization of PTTs around the world, IT suddenly found that they weren't the only game in town. Software as a service (SaaS) gave business users leverage, a weapon, if you like, to choose the solution that best fit their needs, rather than the one that conformed closest to IT standards. Those CIOs who had not looked after their users were more vulnerable to this than those who had. Shadow IT became an increasing problem. The role of the CIO hadn't gone away. It is just that their behavior in not responding to user priorities meant that stakeholders started looking for their answers elsewhere, usually by working with willing and responsive vendors.

Choosing SaaS solutions because IT is not responsive is very short-term thinking. The end to end integration of processes suffers greatly when companies go outside for point solutions without involving IT, the keepers of data models, system resilience, and so on. The point is this; the CIO needs to ensure that IT is properly aligned to the business, now and at all times. It needs to respond to what users want. The new CIO needs to be at the heart of all technical selections. Ian Cox in his book *Disrupt IT*[30] suggests that as part of this role, the CIO moves toward being a services broker, rather than a services provider. Authority and the privilege of position are no longer sufficient for the CIO to retain authority. The new CIO needs to be a salesperson, a diplomat, and a pioneer—in short, the champion of IT.

5.2 A PLAYER, NOT A SPECTATOR

As a corporate player, a successful CIO must fully understand and shape the game plan. Those who work in a competitive/commercial market space need detailed knowledge of the five areas shown in the table below. Those who work for government departments or charities may wish to create the equivalent list for these items. So, equivalent financial metrics for a government organization might include departmental budget and for a charity the source and value of donations, etc.

---

30 Ian Cox, *Disrupt IT,* Amazon Media, 2014

Five Hot Topics	Answers at Your Fingertips
1. The financial metrics and business health of your company	Company turnover Company profitability (before and after tax) Company share price Key operational metrics (and progress to date)
2. The people in your organization	The names of the main board members (and ability to recognize them in the street) The board members' priorities/interests/ background The highest paid employees/salary scales/bonus targets
3. Business strategy	The owner of the corporate strategy (have your access to it) The main corporate objectives The key corporate programs to deliver the strategy The main strategy partners (and their roles) The top three trends that will affect your industry over the next five years
4. Sales and marketing	The top five competitors (or peer organizations) and their relative performance The most recent press articles Sales growth targets for the year ahead Relative importance of different products and markets Upcoming product launches
5. General background	The corporate values Key dates in the organization's history (foundation, acquisitions, major disasters, etc.) The crisis response team members Crisis response plans

TABLE 17. THE FIVE HOT TOPICS OF ORGANIZATIONAL KNOWLEDGE

This information is vital. You should quiz yourself on the details. Vague, high-level knowledge is no longer sufficient. The figures need to be at one's fingertips. The financial metrics should be more than just numbers. Their context must be understood. Is it better or worse than last year, is our profitability better or worse than our competitors, and if so, why? To be good at this, it is also important to have good sources of information, systems that allow you to stay up to date on important information without too much additional research. This is easier said than done. Often, managers are tempted to flood themselves with too much information. But as is often the case in business, less is more. Just focus on the high-level stuff—aim for very good but not for perfection.

5.3 ALIGN IT RESULTS TO THE BUSINESS

In surveys of the priorities of CIOs, aligning IT to the business is the only topic that regularly and repeatedly appears in the top three. At its heart, we can define IT to business alignment as the process of ensuring that IT meets the needs of the business at all levels. In the diagram below, you can see a simplified lifecycle of IT and business development going from left to right. You can also see how processes in the business lifecycle correspond to those in the IT lifecycle. So, there are several points of alignment:

- In the planning stage—IT strategy needs to align to both top-level "corporate" strategy and "functional" (i.e., departmental) strategy.

- In the project phase—IT projects must align to the development of new products and services so that new functionality required for the marketing and sales of these new products and services is embedded in the information systems before they are available for sale in the market.

- In the project phase—IT projects must also be in place to ensure that improvements in business process efficiency are implemented to ensure the business remains fast, responsive, and competitive.

- In the operations phase—Hardware needs to be in place to ensure adequate hardware and network speeds.

- In the operations phase—Security and resilience needs to be in place to ensure that the business is able to conduct operations in a safe and secure way.

- In the results—New projects and improvements in operational performance should deliver improved results for the business and also for IT. IT performance should be measured in terms that have a clear "line of sight" to business success

FIGURE 10. POINTS OF ALIGNMENT FOR IT AND THE BUSINESS

And if you want true alignment, then you will need to align IT to the business at all these points. But of course, there is another complication. Just when you thought you had a good level of alignment, the business goes and changes what it does, and your alignment points change. Work to keep ahead of the game and recognize that perfect alignment is an unattainable goal. The analogy we use is pheasant shooting. If you are trying to shoot a pheasant, aim at where it will be, not where it is now.

5.4 A MODEL FOR IT TO BUSINESS ALIGNMENT

Although it may be an unattainable goal to achieve perfect alignment, it is still vital to have a good model to assess and deliver a closely aligned IT function. The IT team should not only be providing products and services that meet the needs of the business today, but it should also be fully aware of the projected plans of the other business functions, so it can prepare ahead of time for the future.

When we first started our work on alignment, we came across many helpful papers on the subject, identifying what activities are valuable for aligning business and IT. By the time we had finished our research, our list of alignment principles was so long as to be unmanageable. So, we then looked for some common or related themes and, more importantly, a process that might put some structure around it. This model was the result.

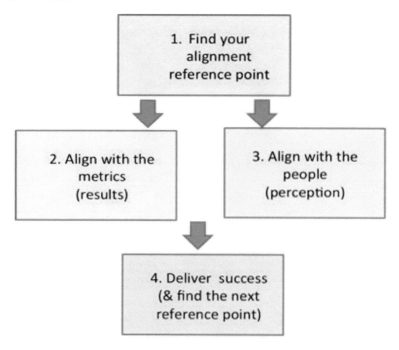

FIGURE 11. A PROCESS FOR ALIGNING IT WITH THE BUSINESS

The model has withstood the test of time. And what we have come to realize is that although most IT managers understand the need for alignment and the sorts of activity that help to bring it about, they are not proactive. And that is why we have the first stage of the process, namely the importance of getting organized and creating the plan.

5.5 CREATE A STRATEGY FOR IT ALIGNMENT

Alignment strategy is not the same as IT strategy but does follow some of the same principles. If you have read *Excellent IT Management*, you will know that the dictionary definition of strategy is a "plan to achieve a long-term aim." In this case, our long-term aim is to achieve business alignment.

There are two important aspects. The first is as simple as recognizing the importance of IT to business alignment and organizing your team to achieve this goal. The best way forward is to think of it as a sales campaign or project. Nominate someone to take ownership of the campaign plan. Before they can create the plan, they will need to know the current situation, with regards to how well IT is currently aligned to the business.

The following guidelines will help you to assess the current situation:

1. Become fully acquainted with the business and get plugged into its high-level strategy

2. Meet with key stakeholders to understand their priorities

3. Get involved in senior decisions via key committees or one-on-one discussions

4. Review your current objectives, and assess where you are in meeting them. Any shortfall should feed directly into any alignment plans you create

From here, you can now create an initial alignment plan. There are two parallel strands, one for aligning the metrics and one for aligning to the people. The people side of alignment includes aligning to senior directors, departmental managers, other key stakeholders, and end users. Aligning the metrics is about "the reality," and the people side is about aligning "perception." Be clear that delivering results may not be, on its own, sufficient for the business to consider that you are well-aligned as an organization.

5.6 ALIGN RESULTS—IT GOVERNANCE

IT governance is the key to aligning IT metrics with business expectations. Governance can be an immensely complex (and dull) business if you let it. And my advice is, don't let it! Over time, we have reviewed a number of governance models, and although rigor is important, so is clarity. Governance structures need to be robust on the one hand and streamlined on the other. Each component needs the right level of authority, responsibility, and competence. Governance structures that hide away all authority at the top level are toothless and inefficient.

Effective IT governance needs the total involvement of the business stakeholders. In their paper, "Six IT Decisions Your IT People Shouldn't Make," Jeanne Ross and Peter Weill[31] identify six particular areas where the business should be specifying what is needed, in effect, setting guidelines for the IT organization to follow.

The six decisions are:

1. How much should we spend on IT?

2. Which business processes should receive our IT dollars?

3. Which IT capabilities need to be companywide?

4. How good do our IT services really need to be?

---

31 "Six IT Decisions Your IT People Shouldn't Make." Jeanne Ross and Peter Weill. *Harvard Business Review*, November, 2002.

5. What security and privacy risks will we accept?

6. Whom do we blame if an IT initiative fails?

Each of these must be addressed as part of IT governance. This will help to define the starting point for the IT strategy and the baseline for IT to deliver. Once under way, we believe that there are four key areas for effective governance and maintaining the alignment between business goals and IT activities.

1. Project performance—reviewing projects through their whole lifecycle, from initial approval to the realization of benefits

2. Performance against targets—ensuring that the IT KPIs are being met and are aligned to the needs of the business. KPI targets also includes financial metrics, such as budget compliance and cost reductions

3. Risk management—providing high-level governance of all risks, not just from individual projects. This includes contingency planning and identifying (potential) black swans

4. Compliance—managing the compliance (and security) requirements of IT and IT's contribution to compliance at the corporate level (Sarbanes Oxley, etc.)

Maintaining these on an ongoing basis is best done through a special governance portal. An example of a governance application is shown below. The top row sets up the reference alignment point. The bottom row shows the four key ongoing alignment and governance activities:

Strategy – setting priorities

Strategy Framework	Goal Setting	Aligning Activity	Resource & Budget
Identify the key areas for strategic emphasis	Set measurable (SMART) business, risk and compliance targets	Create the work plan to meet targets	Estimate the required resources and budget for all activities

Governance – measuring performance

Project Performance	Performance against Targets	Risk Management	Compliance
Monitor and align activities and projects to meeting strategic goals	Review progress towards meeting corporate targets	Monitor progress towards meeting risk mitigation targets	Monitor progress towards meeting compliance objectives

FIGURE 12. AN EXAMPLE APPLICATION FOR MANAGING GOVERNANCE

So, let us look at each of the four:

5.6.1 Project Performance

Most organizations deliver business change through projects. Managing the collection of projects in an organization is known as Project Portfolio Management (PPM). It is vital to choose the right projects and manage investment budgets as wisely as possible. Most companies have a capital approval committee that provides authorization for the projects at the outset but rarely does the same team monitor the projects through to completion. And while it is not essential for the same team to see things through from start to finish, there is certainly a real benefit from continuity. There are many PPM software applications on the market. Choose one that is easy to use and provides useful summary information to evaluate progress.

The following guidelines are our guidelines for successful PPM:

1. Implement a PPM system that tracks project performance through its whole lifecycle, from initial investment approval, to close down with an assessment of the realization of benefits.

2. Arrange for the project board to meet regularly enough to contribute but not too often that it becomes too much of an overhead (and senior execs stop attending).

3. Keep the project board membership at a high level, with not too many participants (to avoid discussions being protracted).

4. Assign a senior manager to be responsible for running the project board. This manager should have access to other board members on an ad hoc basis between meetings to make sure that background work is done on major issues prior to the board meeting, rather than during.

5. Make the project board meetings interesting. Don't forget to remind the group of successful projects and how they are changing the way the business operates.

5.6.2 Performance Against Targets

Most organizations are used to setting objectives and measuring their ongoing performance with a set of Key Performance Indicators (KPIs). These objectives should ensure that the IT organization is delivering to the needs and priorities of the business. They should address each of the four areas of the Balanced Scorecard, namely, the customer (i.e., users and customers for IT departments), process (we also include technology in this), people, and finance. The following are some examples of metrics from organizations we have worked with. IT organizations would have just a few key metrics from each quadrant.

Users & Business Sponsors	IT Process & Technology
User satisfaction (inc. quality of communication)	Project lifecycle time
Call answer time / first time fix rates	Number of projects delivered (successfully)
Demand management (time to respond)	Systems reliability, scalability & availability
% Business requests directed to IT	Total number of outages (different priorities)
Response to requests (IMAC's)	Quality of deliverables (bug rates)
Easier to use systems / More integrated	Major incident levels / measured impact
Easier for the customer	Number of changes implemented
Speed of response (user terminal)	Number of platforms / architectural changes
Accuracy e.g. Billing, reporting	Level of security / compliance

IT Team / Management	Financial
Skills development	Benefit realization
Staff retention	Capital & operational expense
Average salary	Number of suppliers and contract value
Training investment	Sourcing / outsource
Teamwork	IT asset / stock levels / utilization (mobile vs. fixed)
Utilization	Governance & decision making
Employee survey	
Organizational improvement	
Internal to external staff ratio	

FIGURE 13. EXAMPLES OF IT METRICS ACROSS A BALANCED SCORECARD

Some of the process objectives will be set through Service Level Agreements. SLAs can be a valuable tool. A couple of key points, though, regarding SLAs. One of the six key decisions Jeanne Ross and Peter Weill identified was, "How good do our IT services really need to be?" Clearly, perfection in all areas is not attainable, but the other extreme is potentially more dangerous.

So, the first point about SLAs, is to be clear that the senior stakeholders and the end users really do sign off on the SLA levels being described. If the business wants a service level higher than the bare minimum, then they should probably have it, otherwise resentment will grow. Secondly, when an SLA is set, the IT organization should not be afraid to exceed it. Sometimes an SLA is used as an excuse for poor service. IT aims to hit the SLA straight on, rather than exceed expectations. Culturally, this is a road to nowhere. What other department aims to deliver exactly the minimum acceptable service?

5.6.3 Risk and Compliance

Most organizations are very good at managing risks at a project level. This is discussed in detail in *Excellent IT Management*. However, for effective IT governance, risk should also be managed at the corporate level. Some of the risks at this level may include the most severe risks from the individual projects. But a different approach is also needed for top-level risk management. First of all, the risks being discussed are often those that have a more severe impact on the overall business.

At a corporate level, you may wish to consider risks at four levels:

1. What are the major risks in the IT strategic plan?

2. What are the major risks inhibiting our key projects?

3. What are the major risks to our operational integrity?

4. What are the major risks impacting compliance and security?

When working through this, it is important to focus on the top risks. The most successful organizations work on a list of five or ten top risks. Plans are put in place to mitigate the risks, and when the size of the risk is reduced sufficiently, another risk will rise up the list, which can then be worked on. Focusing on fewer risks means that meaningful work can be done rather than spreading the available resources too thinly.

In *Excellent IT Management*, we also looked at a number of techniques for addressing risks. Without going into detail, the techniques covered:

1. Traditional risk management—looking at probability vs. impact

2. Assumption-based risk management—an effective technique that looks at the assumption base of risks, widening the discussion, and effectively providing a more accurate assessment of risk

3. Quality-based costing and Monte Carlo analysis—a techniques for quantifying which risks are having the greater impact on the successful delivery (in terms of time and cost) for a project and identifying the most valuable activities to mitigate risk

There is a final technique that is not mentioned, and that is to do with "black swans." Black swans were first brought to light by Nassim Nicholas Taleb[32] in his book of the same name. He proposed that organizations should be able to withstand "difficult to predict" events. A black swan is basically a phenomenon that seemed implausible before it happened, but once it happened, it seemed entirely predictable.

Traditional risk management techniques are not very good at predicting black swans. It does need a slightly different and focused approach. In *Excellent IT Management*, we looked at two components of risk, namely sensitivity and stability measured as follows:

Sensitivity
How sensitive are you to the assumption/what will be the impact if the assumption proves untrue?
A = Minor Impact (not sensitive)
B = Manageable Impact
C = Significant Impact
D = Critical Impact (very sensitive)

Stability
How confident are you that the assumption will turn out to be stable/ true (without taking additional actions)?
A = Very confident (stable)
B = Fairly confident
C = Uncomfortable
D = Very uncomfortable (unstable)

---

32 *The Black Swan, The Impact of the Highly Improbable*, Nassim Nicholas Taleb, Penguin, 2008.

Plotting them on the matrix below, you can see that most traditional risk management focuses on the biggest risks, in other words, those that you are highly sensitive to (high impact) with unstable assumptions (quite probable). These are shown in the top-right quadrant of Diagram 3 below.

Black swans are those events that are considered unlikely to happen, but if they were to happen, would have a serious impact. In other words, high impact, but (initially) considered to be very unlikely (stable assumptions). The art of identifying black swans is to look at your risks in the bottom-right quadrant and evaluate them from a different viewpoint. On closer inspection, you may find that in fact the stability of the assumption is flawed and that they need to be addressed as a more serious risk.

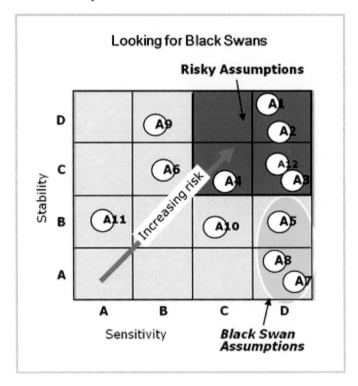

FIGURE 14. LOOKING FOR BLACK SWANS

A final word on compliance. It is important to know what level of compliance you are seeking. Legal compliance regulations set minimum standards for compliance in many areas. Attaining these goals is not an option. But in some cases, there is some subjectivity. So, the question is, who decides what the right level should be? Returning to the paper of Jeanne Ross and Peter Weill, the answer is the business. The business should decide what is acceptable. All too often, it is the auditors who decide. I have come across situations where an organization worked hard to comply with audit recommendations one year. During the following months, the company changed their auditors, and IT needed to undertake significant additional work to meet a new set of audit requirements. The point is not that the standards get higher year after year, which may also be true, but that consideration should be given as to what is really needed.

5.6.4 IT Governance Structures

Figure 15 below gives an example of an IT governance structure. Although we have amended this over a couple of years with input from delegates, no one size fits all. The shape of the model should reflect the shape of your business. The next section gives some examples of how different business set up their governance to give an idea of different structures. The model emphasizes that you need the right governance forums *and* the right people in charge. Using the color key in the model below, you can see that the senior management should be leading the IT steering group, the capital committee, the compliance committee, and the project board (shown in blue). The other groups can be led by the CIO or by other IT managers. These responsibilities are only guidelines. The IT technology and innovation council, for example, is shown as the responsibility of the CIO. It does indeed provide an excellent leadership opportunity for the CIO to lead innovation in an organization. However, some organizations have their own chief innovation officers, and it would be reasonable to assume that they would run this meeting. Conversely, the chart suggests that the Crisis Response Team should be led by a non-IT senior executive. In fact, in many cases, it is the CIO who is the chairperson.

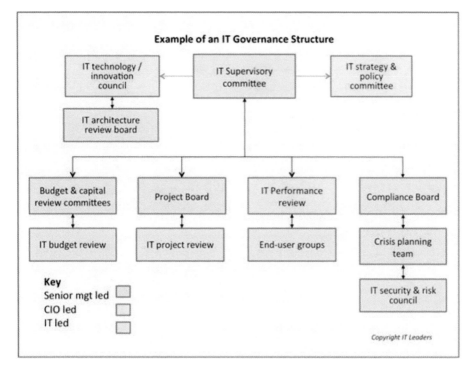

FIGURE 15. EXAMPLE OF AN IT GOVERNANCE STRUCTURE

5.7 TEN EXAMPLES OF GOVERNANCE

The objective of the section is to show the thinking and principles that a number of organizations used to set up their governance. No two organizations are the same, but hopefully understanding different case examples may help you with your own.

Governance is an important part of any IT department. It ensures that the investment goes to the right projects, ensures that IT is operating efficiently, and protects the organization is security and other risks. It is a serious subject, and you won't need to read many articles on the subject to realize that there are few laughs in IT governance. What I would say is that if it gets really tedious, it probably means that it is being done in too much detail (too many long meetings with lots of participants, rather than smaller groups) or structured incorrectly or that authority is not properly delegated down. Governance, for whatever reason, has become a repository for management-speak. Maybe together, we can start a campaign to bring clear and simple language to the world of governance and save it from itself. Jargon and complex language can obscure the reality and makes it difficult to make the necessary decisions for IT's success.

The ten examples in this chapter describe a wide range of governance structures. Each situation is different, but they also have a number of things in common. To be effective, good governance needs:

1. A structure that reflects the shape and priorities of the business with authority and responsibility delegated down to the correct level. A business run with separate divisions reporting to a head office function would have governance at the divisional level as well as the corporate level, for example. Some will require something much simpler.

2. Good people who have good knowledge of the technical aspects, as well as good communications skills. Some naysayers have remarked this rather limits the list of possible candidates. Nonetheless, a good governance structure will not work if the people who have the authority are not suitably qualified and do not fully understand the implications of the decisions they are making. The governance members also need to be very clear on what their individual responsibilities are and take them seriously. One CIO created a statement for each governance board member to sign, which explained their specific role. This avoids the problem of "governance tourism," where committee members turn up to meetings for the ride and assume that someone else will take care of the specifics.

3. A governance body whose members have a good working view of the IT architecture. This does not mean detailed technical diagrams but a high-level enterprise type architecture or clear schematics that explain the different IT entities in a useful format.

4. An understanding by the governance members of the business strategy, the priorities, and objectives of the key divisions and departments of the organization.

5. A clear understanding of what IT governance should achieve. In my experience, there are two types of achievements—those that are statutory, permanent objectives that an IT governance framework should meet and those that are current objectives. The structure may well change according to current problems that are being encountered within IT. For example, one IT company we worked with was encountering problems with departments working on non-sanctioned projects (officially called "shadow IT") but unofficially known as "skunk works" in the UK. The governance framework was amended to address this. Members of each business unit were required to be part of the governance process and were held accountable for unapproved work. It only took one course of disciplinary action to change the behavior of the business.

6. A need to assure the security of the IT systems and manage the important risks.

7. And finally, it needs to be clear and complete. In particular, it needs to cover all aspects of governance in a structured way, so that everything is covered in one place and one place only. It should summarize information as it goes from one level to the next level up, so that the top level has a complete accurate and clear picture of the overall state of governance.

In order to achieve the last of these goals, it is important to create an outline of the relative roles and responsibilities of your governance structure and publish it. One of the main causes of bureaucracy in governance is where roles are duplicated across different parts of the governance structure, and the lines of responsibility are blurred. The following table gives a high-level example of how this might be done. In practice, you will probably also need to add more detail. In particular, it is important that each organization has its own charter, essentially a description of what it is responsible for, what it can and cannot decide, and who (or which committee) to escalate to for what type of issue.

GOVERNANCE ORGANIZATION	FUNCTION	OWNER	MOST SENIOR REPRESENTATIVE
IT supervisory committee	Provides top level guidance and decisions for the IT organization based on input from other groups	CIO	Chief executive
Technology innovation council	Assesses opportunities for new technologies and signs off architectural road-map	Chief architect	CIO
IT strategy and policy committee	Reviews IT strategy against possible options and signs off IT policies in all areas, including security	Head of IT strategy	CIO
Budget and capital review committees	Reviews all business cases and approves annual budget (in line with strategy). May be part of company-wide capital committee, but IT checkpoints should be in place	CIO	CFO
Project board	Agrees project prioritization, assesses project risk and provides resource where required	Head of IT projects Programme Office	CEO or CIO
IT performance review	Reviews IT operational performance, e.g. incident level, major incident response, change control and other IT specific metrics	Head of IT operations	CIO
IT compliance board –	Supervises compliance of IT to all legislation and standards (may report to higher, company-wide boards	Head of compliance / Head of security	CIO / Head of audit

TABLE 18. EXAMPLE OF GOVERNANCE ROLES AND RESPONSIBILITIES

Richard Nolan and Warren McFarlan in their paper "Information Technology and the Board of Directors"[33] suggested that two components had particular importance in how organizations should set up their IT governance. The first aspect was the criticality of the information system (i.e., where there is a loss of business if the systems fail for a minute or more) and the need for new/innovative IT solutions. These two axes gave four types they called the IT Strategic Impact Grid. They suggested guidelines for each of the four quadrants. In the examples below, you will see that our experience matches their findings in several cases.

5.7.1 A Small or Medium Enterprise (SME)

The important criterion for an SME is efficiency. Many SMEs do not have their own IT department and rely on external providers for their information systems. But just because IT does not sit in the organization does not mean the board of directors can abdicate responsibility for governance. It will count for little if any supplier suffers a DNS attack or breach of security. The company still needs contingency plans in place. One training

---

33 Richard Nolan and Warren McFarlan, "Information Technology and the Board of Directors," *Harvard Business Review*, October 2005.

company we worked with (not IT Leaders, although we did have similar difficulties when we went to a cloud-based accounting solution!) went to an online sales management solution. They were so convinced by the size and track record of this supplier that they assumed the system migration would go smoothly. In reality, it was far from that. The company was without sales reporting figures for three months, something that was crippling for the business.

Still, in terms of the governance structure, a simple one will suffice, perhaps with just one decision board. It is recommended that IT strategy and governance is done separately and not as part of the regular board meeting to avoid directors getting distracted. The meeting should include one or two outside experts as well as representatives of the key suppliers. Outside experts are vital to give a view of the market (independent from the key suppliers). A word of caution—just because two independent experts agree, doesn't necessarily make them right!

Key subjects for the meeting are:

- Are we getting the performance we require from our suppliers?

- Have we assessed the key IT risks and put plans in to mitigate them?

- Do we know the product roadmap for the products we use, and when would we plan to upgrade to new versions?

5.7.2 A Research Company

Research companies need to be able to take on new systems in order to stay at the forefront of their industry. Production systems are typically less important, so the emphasis tends to be away from high availability. Even so, security is important, so they needed good and robust operational effectiveness.

In this example, the company CIO was concerned that the senior executive was not involved enough in IT. The problem was good and bad.

The CEO, in particular, was happy that IT was being run well and had turned his attention to other parts of the business. The CIO was worried, though, because he was seeing that almost all of the projects currently in the portfolio were for enterprise type systems and almost none for research systems. His view was that if they neglected research systems, there was a danger that their competitive advantage would be eroded. The company already had an IT board, but over time, it had become primarily concerned with KPIs, status of projects under way. and performance against budget. And as a result, the MD had stopped attending.

The solution in this case was the formation of a new IT innovation board that included the most influential board members, including the heads of research departments. This helped to solve this problem, since the CIO could focus effort on the business and the priorities of research. A consequence of this was that the main IT board meetings had more purpose and the MD became reengaged.

5.7.3 A Manufacturing Company

The manufacturing company in this example was a multi-national company, making different types of equipment in its different factories. Each division had a different manufacturing process. A number of the divisions had been acquired and initially had different finance, reporting, and even e-mail systems. Over time, the financial systems had been consolidated. Production, manufacturing, and in most cases, service and support systems were different for each division.

One of the key criteria for governance was identifying which systems needed to be handled centrally and which ones were unique to each operation. Politics were quite important. Each divisional manager tried to run their own business autonomously and were reluctant to have corporate systems "slowing them down." The problem was that costs had escalated, and it was becoming increasing vital to share expertise and create cross-divisional synergy. Matters were not helped by head office bundling excessive and unnecessary costs into the charge-backs.

The first step in solving the governance was to recognize that it would never be possible for all divisions to have the same systems. The structure was set up with one overall IT governance board. Feeding this was a divisional IT governance board. The head of each divisional board (usually the divisional CIO or general manager or both) then attended the overall board. There was also a corporate systems IT board (generally attended by all the divisional CIOs). A key success factor in this case was a simplified systems architecture that showed which systems were central and which could be distributed, sometimes called the "wedding cake diagram."[34]

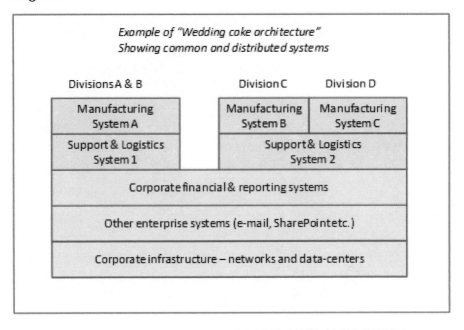

FIGURE 16. AN EXAMPLE OF A "WEDDING CAKE" ARCHITECTURE

The policy guidelines were important here. Even though the divisions had full control over their manufacturing systems, the corporate organization recommended standards and solutions that should be considered. Over time, more than half of the divisions were using the same production applications, even if their implementations were different. The

---

34 Developed from an idea by the Leading Edge Forum, an information technology research and advisory services company.

governance structure also had teeth. If a divisional general manager was not following the policy, then there were sanctions. It is not enough to have a good governance structure. Governance needs to be carried out in a disciplined way.

5.7.4 A Company with Outsourced IT

On the surface, outsourcing IT might appear to be the simplest way to avoid the puzzle of IT governance. Of course, this is very far from reality. In fact, IT governance becomes even more important for companies that have outsourced their IT.

Although most companies will have laid out clear governance structures in their contract, it is commonplace to transfer too many staff to the outsourcing partner for them to carry out their obligations. It is absolutely vital to retain key and highly experienced IT staff to properly manage the relationship.

It makes better commercial sense for the outsource partner if they can keep as much control over the information systems for themselves. Without a proper client oversight function, critical information is often held back. For example, how many staff are actually working on the outsource contract? Are there areas that could be made more efficient and save money? In fact, the list is endless. One large auto manufacturer we worked with recently had almost no visibility of their outsource partner's resources assigned to their account. The correct numbers were clearly laid out in the contract, but since the oversight function was lacking, no one had actually checked.

Pay particular attention to the type and quantity of reporting. It is very common for outsource companies to provide a plethora of reports that the oversight function cannot properly assess. It is critical that the reports are clearly specified, show only summarized detail, and *very, very* clearly state what the problems are and what is being done to resolve them. A final word on governing outsource partners. Never give too much responsibility to one party. You should always be able to "walk the

corridors." This means you have the ability to know where your work is being carried out and for you to have free access to it at any time.

5.7.5 An International Law Firm

One client, an international law firm, has a different approach to IT governance. In this case, IT is very valuable to the organization, but is not really a source of competitive advantage. Although it would be inconvenient for the systems to go down, it is unlikely that significant revenue will be lost. Law firms, like many professional service firms, have a large number of partners, each of whom owns a part of the firm and has a vested interest in its success. This can cause some problems, as each partner can often feel that they can make unilateral decisions about particular aspects of IT.

In this case, the firm assigned one (enthusiastic) young partner to head up the IT governance board. She was responsible for liaising with the CIO, basically acting as a single point of contact for the lawyers. She set up one main governance board (called the IT steering committee). This essentially combined many of the aspects of the governance chart in Figure 15, in particular the strategy, architecture, innovation, and budget. Security and compliance was handled through the firm's robust audit function. Supplier management was handled on a supplier by supplier basis. Sourcing strategy, of course, was handled by the IT steering committee.

The day-to-day IT operational issues were handled by the CIO who had an additional responsibility to bring any exceptions to the IT steering committee when he thought it appropriate. This separation of the strategic from the operational allowed the IT partner to keep governance manageable and spend time on her day job. Having a responsible partner was particularly helpful in the implementation of important change initiatives, where the lawyers could see that these were now being led by the law firm, rather than by IT.

One particular problem that comes to mind was difference of opinion over storage management. The partners found it very difficult to understand why anyone should pay any attention to keeping storage under certain thresholds. "For heaven's sake," said one partner, "I can go down the store and buy one terabyte of storage for eighty dollars, so why do we need to manage it? If we charged for the time spent arguing about it, we could have bought a hundred already!" It was problems like this that the IT partner was able to resolve. In this particular case, it was emphasizing the importance of confidentiality and resilience and having the key information available to those who needed it, rather than the cost.

5.7.6 Financial Services

Governance in the financial services sector is a particularly complex puzzle, requiring strong controls and compliance with a number of industry specific standards. It is too detailed a subject for this book. However, anyone interested in this would do well in the first instance to read the paper "Linking Strategy, IT governance and Performance"[35] by Peter Weill and Jeanne W. Ross. This paper is excerpted from *IT Governance: How Top Performers Manage IT Decision Rights for Superior Results.*[36]

This article describes their model for IT governance design, based on the following six principles:

1. Enterprise strategy and organization

2. IT governance arrangements

3. Business performance goals

4. IT organization and desirable behaviors

5. IT metrics and accountabilities

6. IT governance mechanisms

---

35 Peter Weill, Jeanne W. Ross, "Linking Strategy, IT Governance and Performance," *Harvard Business Press*, ISBN-13:978-1-8092-1.

36 Peter Weill, Jeanne W. Ross, *IT Governance: How Top Performers Manage IT Decision Rights for Superior Results,* Harvard Business Review Press, 2004.

Their work is supported by two case studies from JPMorgan Chase and State Street Corporation.

5.7.7 A Telecoms Turnaround

A clear principle of IT governance is that it needs to fit the organization. This does not just mean the organizational structure but also the market environment. A company that is going through rapid change requires a highly responsive and agile framework that provides an appropriate balance between assuring quality and responding to changing market needs. An Asian cable media company we worked with provides a good example. The organization had grown through acquisition and had four different systems architectures spread over the different regions, not dissimilar, in fact, to the distributed systems of the production manufacturing system of Example 3. However, there was a huge opportunity to rationalize the systems to one common architecture. Although this would save costs, the real driver was to provide a single view of the customer. In the old systems, a customer who had bought more than one product appeared as a separate customer for each product in the Customer Relationship Management systems and again in the billing systems.

Because all of the divisions and process owners had to work so closely together, all of the strategy was developed through one top-level strategy committee. The CIO worked with each of the department heads outside of the strategy board meetings to build the IT strategy that was then reviewed by the board.

A transformation project was put in place. Seventy percent of the corporate IT budget was assigned to this project. Because of its immense strategic importance to the company, the CEO headed up the program board. Divisional general managers were also members of the board, and since the CEO was chairing it, they were invariably present! Other projects were handled by the CIO as part of a bi-weekly project portfolio meeting. Partner governance was handled on a case-by-case basis. Security and continuity planning was led by the head of IT operations.

This governance structure worked well during the implementation. Once the implementation was complete, the structure was changed to match the new shape of the business. All projects were handled through the bi-weekly portfolio meetings, but this was then chaired by the chief operating officer who took over from the CIO.

5.7.8 A Government Department

The governance of IT within government is a very serious business. The Obama Care systems failure is a good case in point, where insufficient planning and controls (among other things) meant that the system was unable to cope with the volume of activity when it went live. In 2011 in the UK, it was announced that an ambitious program, costing over fifteen billion dollars, to create a computerized patient record system across the entire National Health Service (NHS) was being scrapped. It would not be fair to suggest that better governance would have solved all problems. Nonetheless, better oversight would have paid closer attention and certainly could have reduced the amount wasted. In fact, in the case of the NHS system, there was nothing to suggest that the governance structure was flawed. Unfortunately, good governance structures by themselves do not ensure good governance. The process needs to be run by experienced and capable people.

ISO 38500 (also known by its official title of ISO/IEC 38500:2008)[37] is the international standard for the corporate governance of IT. It is a high-level, principles-based advisory standard and provides broad guidelines on the role of a governing body. The first task of anyone who works a government department is to obtain the existing IT governance standard and become fully briefed on how it is implemented and how it relates to your own responsibilities.

The international standard is based on six principles, not dissimilar to the model put forward earlier in this chapter. To make it useful and practical, these principles need to be extended to match the priorities and

---

37 Corporate Governance of Information Technology, ISO/IEC 38500:2008, originally prepared by Standards Australia (as AS8015:2005).

requirements of that department. The six principles are as follows (the interpretation is mine—refer to the standard itself for the exact wording):

1. Principle of Responsibility—Responsibility and authority need to be in the same place.

2. Principle of Strategy—Business strategy looks at current and future requirements and ensures business and IT are aligned.

3. Principle of Acquisition—IT acquisitions have to follow a structured and transparent process. There needs to be a proper business case that takes proper account of all costs and project risks.

4. Principle of Performance—Service levels need to be in place that meet the needs of the organization, and those standards need to be adhered to.

5. Principle of Conformance—IT must comply with appropriate mandatory legislation and regulations (external). Policies and working practices are clearly laid out and also complied with (internal).

6. Principle of Human Behavior—IT policies, practices, and decisions are respectful of those who are impacted by IT—both the IT department and IT users. This aspect is not part of our governance model and, in our experience, is usually handled by the human resources department

5.7.9 A Logistics Company

For a logistics company, the focus was not so much on fast change but on continually improving operational performance. Logistics companies work in a particularly difficult environment. The business demands the highest of standards. In this particular case, the company had gone through a significant growth period, as it took on capacity to handle the large growth in parcels delivery as a result of Internet sales. Over the last few years, though, the systems have successfully scaled to meet the higher volumes, and the business products have remained relatively stable. Even so, the business is intolerant of any errors in processing, and even though systems were not always to blame for lost parcels, detailed reporting and data mining solutions are an essential tool to continually improve performance.

With regard to governance, therefore, the company focuses on key performance indicators around system uptime, network response, reliability, and business continuity. Although the company operates internationally, the highly optimized processes are at the heart of its success and standardized across country borders (with some variations for import duty, customs regulations, tax, currency, and so on). The role of governance is therefore to optimize efficiency and use the learning from different countries to continually improve. Governance sits at the top (corporate) level, bringing together ideas from the regions. Feeding into the IT board is an operational excellence committee that also has the innovation remit for continual improvement. The project board for IT projects is chaired by the CIO with representatives from the regions. The head of operations is a member of the company-wide business continuity team that reports to the head of audit and security.

5.7.10 A Charity

We have worked with several charities. No two operate in the same way, and their governance processes reflect this. To try and generalize, though, it is probably fair to say that the majority of the information systems are important but not mission critical. Website performance can be a particular concern as charity websites can often be subject to huge spikes. Television appeals, for example, can sometimes cause huge surges in interest (from relief agencies to rehousing animals), and robust and scalable systems are necessary.

Many medium to larger charities also tend to have large numbers of people in the field, including volunteers, as well as employees. Access to the information systems in these cases needs to be reliable but also easy to use. The governance of IT needs to take this into consideration.

Charities also have some uniqueness in that many of those involved in their top-level governance come from outside the charity itself (for example, major benefactors) and often from different walks of life. Charities in general seem to be particularly subject to outside scrutiny. As a result, it can be difficult for them to get a breadth of production level IT expertise on the IT board. It makes good sense to be a little bit streetwise and debate IT issues in detail in the equivalent of an internal IT board before presenting findings and conclusions to any external body. There is also a strong case to appoint a senior external IT expert to the board of governors to support IT in its proposals.

5.8 ALIGN PEOPLE TO ENHANCE PERCEPTION

So far, we have looked at the results side of IT to business alignment and focused particularly on the importance of good governance structures and processes to ensure that IT is delivering the right solutions for the business. This takes care of the "reality" of the situation. But every experienced IT manager will know that delivering good results is often not enough. It is important to take care of the "perception" of the stakeholders and users. Users are not interested just in results but how those results are delivered. IT managers need a plan to look after the perception of their performance.

In a recent survey, it was found that the main drivers of effective alignment were as follows.

- Senior executives support IT

- IT involved in strategy development

- IT understands the business

- IT and non-IT have close relationship

- IT shows strong leadership

- IT efforts are well-prioritized

- IT meets commitments

You can see from this list that the top five factors were to do with the people side of alignment, rather than the results/governance side. It is vital that the IT organization stays plugged in to all parts of the organization at all levels.

Think about how far your influence spreads through your organization and how you might improve it. If you go back to the structure from the previous section, you will see that there are many players involved in the successful governance of IT. That leaves many opportunities for miscommunication and misunderstanding. Think about where this is most likely to happen. Perhaps there are key players who you do not know very well or who are not well-disposed to the work that IT is doing. Include these people when you create your plan. The plan should be coordinated by your IT alignment manager. In other words, contacts with key players should be managed carefully. Meetings with them should be coordinated so they are well known to a number of managers in your department but not so many as they are overwhelmed with attention. Your plan should show how you match up your managers with the key managers in the business.

I once worked in an organization with a number of service directors, each of whom was assigned to a divisional director. These managers were very experienced and reported to me as the CIO. The divisional directors liked the dedicated contact, but unfortunately the service directors did not always have the authority to act on what they were being asked for. This created a conflict (basically they were overpromising), as well as providing me with a significant management overhead. We quickly reorganized, so the department was segmented along divisional lines, which was also broadly how the systems and processes were organized. This meant that that we now had the authority and responsibility in the same part of the organization. This benefitted the divisional directors who (generally) got what they wanted. It was also highly motivating for the service directors, who were now empowered to deliver (it also curbed their desire to overpromise!)

Take opportunities to consult regularly with the business. Use feedback questionnaires on a regular basis and respond to comments quickly, however insignificant they may seem. If users take the time to give feedback and then find their comments are not acted on, it becomes increasingly difficult to get their commitment in the future and only adds to a feeling that IT is not aligned to the business.

SCOTT'S STORY: GOOD SERVICE, BAD PERCEPTION

I was working in Houston for an oil services company. We had a large IT department with a set of proven and robust IT processes. Systems reliability was vital and we invested heavily in training our people on the procedures. One day I received a call from our CEO who informed me that his laptop appeared to have lost all the data on its hard drive. He had left it with one of our technicians to upgrade to operating system while he was in a meeting. When he returned, he was unable to access the data.

I passed the call on to our head of desk side support who allocated our top man to the job. About 20 minutes later, I saw him in the car park having a quick cigarette. My first reaction was that this was good news and assumed that the problem had just been a simple user error. Unfortunately this was not the case. When I asked him what the problem had been he looked at me blankly. "I haven't looked at it yet," he told me. "The SLA is 30 minutes and I still have time to finish my cigarette!"

Worse than that. It turned out not to be a user error. We really had forgotten to back up his data. And the fact that the CEO had also seen our expert outside did nothing to enhance his perception of IT. Although the business had signed the SLA that we were working to, they did not agree with it. Even if we exceeded the SLA, and in theory met our targets, it did not mean the business was happy. And the fact that we were aiming our sights to match it as closely as possible was singularly unhelpful. As I said to my team, it is a bit like entering the high jump and aiming to knock off the bar. It took many months to change this paradigm and for our team to realize that it is not just what you do, but how you do it.

Get knowledgeable people out in the field speaking to users. It may be that your most knowledgeable people are not particularly good in face-to-face discussions. One of my managers used to say that these people "did not have a very good user interface!" If you have staff like this, don't send them out unprotected. Provide them with training and coaching to develop their skills, and have one of your more customer-friendly managers work with them in their meetings. In fact, it is one of the most common feedback responses we receive from delegates, that training all IT people to be customer focused and customer friendly is one of the most important aspects of successful alignment.

Finally, pay particular attention to senior management. If you have a well-structured campaign to work with your IT managers so they have contacts and presence across the whole organization, it is essential that the IT director takes the leading role in working with the senior executives. It is the role of the senior IT executives in general and the IT director in particular to teach the business about IT. This should be done for all senior managers, emphasizing the point that politics should be avoided at all costs. One CIO I interviewed used to run a technology showcase once a year. It provided an opportunity for his team to put together a collection of new and interesting technologies that might be of value to the organization but also provided an opportunity to discuss with the board members where they were in terms of the adoption of existing and new technologies. It also provided an opportunity to show the senior managers the achievements of the IT team working with the business over the previous period.

6. Secrets of Success

6.1 THE IT LEADERS TOP TEN LIST

THIS BOOKS COVERS A LOT OF GROUND. SO, OF ALL THE THINGS WE HAVE COVERED, WHAT ARE THE TEN THINGS THAT CIOS BELIEVE make the biggest difference to their career success? The following was compiled from our work with CIOs:

1. Spend time with key influencers—Networking is vital for building the CIO's profile, for promoting innovation, solving interdepartmental problems, and influencing strategy to name but a few. When my colleague, Dr. Robina Chatham, did her research on successful CIOs, she found that some of them claimed to spend over half of their time on networking. This may be a reflection of what you and I might call soothing frustrated users, they call networking. The point is clear, though. Every interaction with others in the business is an opportunity to solve problems and build influence. The expression, "Be courteous with people and ruthless with time," is very apt in this context. Effective CIOs build better networks because they recognize some people carry more influence than others. And they pay particular attention to two of them—their boss and their boss's boss.

2. Create and communicate clear strategy—Strategy is defined as "a plan to achieve a long-term aim." So, be clear on the long-term aim, and create a plan to achieve it! Avoid detailed analysis in the

creation of strategy. Put projects and activities in place to deliver the objectives and resource them properly. Finally, spend time creating a clear and concise strategy presentation that business sponsors and stakeholders can understand and embrace.

3. Create a clear business and technology roadmap—It is vital for a CIO to have an understanding of the changing business environment and clear opinion as to how technology will evolve to meet it. Using the techniques of Chapter 5, think about which technologies have application for your business and how they might be deployed. Create a "time-lapse" view in your mind of how the IT infrastructure will change, how the business applications will develop, and how the IT function will adapt to the future over the next three, five, and ten years. Finally, stay close to new initiatives, surveying the project landscape for potential business change problems. Your role as an IT leader is to coach the business sponsors to understand and resolve business change issues.

4. Align the priorities of IT with the business—IT to business alignment has been in the top three priorities of CIOs for over twenty years; it has been important for a long time and doesn't look like it's going out of style anytime soon. Aligning with today's priorities isn't necessarily enough. You need good visibility of where the future lies, so you can aim your IT at the right target. IT objectives should be aligned, not only to the top-level corporate objectives but also to the other departmental objectives. Your team should have a line of sight to your objectives, so that everyone is working in the same direction. Set up good governance to support alignment efforts. Governance should match the shape of your organization. Roles and responsibilities should be clearly defined with a minimum of overlap. It should be set up to choose good projects and motivate senior management to stay closely involved in their delivery.

5. Ensure the right level of risk and security—IT staff will always do their best to create a secure and risk-free environment. However, perfect security is not an achievable goal, and business leaders need

to join with IT managers to identify the objectives and ambitions of security. Everyone needs to be realistic about risks and know that the best way to reduce it is to properly understand and act on it. Risk is about probability and impact. So, although you may have good processes set up for reducing the probability of things going wrong, sooner or later, they still will. Have a practiced team in place for handling crises. There is nothing like a badly handled IT crisis to force a CIO's resignation.

6. Create an innovation culture—Continuous improvement is in the DNA of IT people. IT departments need to understand the importance of doing new things and making the old ones better. IT employees need to be asking a lot of questions—why are we doing this, and how can we do it better? IT leadership needs to be creating the right working environment, providing good sources of technology information, embedding innovation in the objectives of the team, and encouraging innovation workshops with business stakeholders.

7. Develop the skills and aspirations of the IT team—Any IT leader needs to be motivating and inspiring their team to achieve their best. Money, according to the surveys, is not the biggest motivational factor. Team members are much more energized by working on interesting projects and being recognized by their managers and the top executives. So, make sure they are!

8. Create a user-friendly organization—So many talented CIOs have moved on in a hurry because they ran out of friends. An IT department that is friendly to its sponsors, stakeholders, and users will find it has friends to help when it needs them most. Making IT processes easy to use, friendly, and informative is one of many important priorities for the CIO. Showing the business that you are listening and agile in moving to solve problems is vital for long-term success. CIOs who spend the shortest time in the role are those who do not provide the highest levels of support for their senior executives. It is tempting to have one level of service for all. Unfortunately, the reality of business is such that if you do not

have proper executive support, you will waste precious leadership opportunities listening to the board's problems with laptops and tablet PCs! The perception of people, as well as the reality of results, is vital to success.

9. Find and nurture good technology partners—In the new, disrupted world of IT, organizations have come to rely more and more on their vendors to support them. No longer are IT departments writing their own programs from scratch. IT vendors have off-the-shelf solutions for every client. CIOs need to think carefully about what they keep in house and what can be outsourced based on strategic importance and strike the right balance. And, when choosing strategic partners, choose good ones, partners who understand your business, provide high-quality service, and act as a source of innovation and competitive advantage.

10. Promote your brand—A CIO with a good brand that inspires confidence in the business can get things done much more easily than one without. But not everything is about the business. At some time, the CIO needs to think about themselves. They need to think about their profile and brand outside the organization, too. One day, you will be looking for a new role. It is vital to have a good network outside your organization that includes technology partners, peer organizations, headhunters, and industry bodies. Brand is about many things, but nothing is as important as leadership. Change your time profile, so you are spending more time on quadrant two leadership activities. You should promote yourself as the corporate IT leader and be seen by everyone as part of the business, not part of IT.

6.2 INGREDIENTS OF WORLD-CLASS IT

In Chapter 2, we looked at the key components of effective IT team management. At first sight, it seems logical to believe that an effectively managed IT team makes for an effective IT team. This is not the case. The truth is that effective IT team management does not, per se, make for

an effective IT team. And the reason we mention it now is that it needs many of the principles described in different parts of this book (as well as *Excellent IT Management*) to come together. It is the ultimate task of the corporate IT leader.

Our work with IT organizations suggested that it requires much more than good management to create a great IT capability. Although the team management factors described in this chapter are an essential component of IT team success, the nirvana of a world-class IT capability means solving a much more complex puzzle. Over the last three years, we have put together a model to assess all of the factors for an effective IT team. The result is shown below:

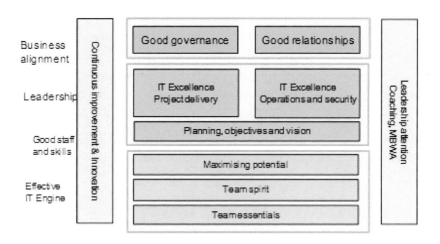

FIGURE 17. THE INGREDIENTS OF WORLD-CLASS IT

In the model, you can see that there are ten ingredients. The bottom three, shown in green, represent the IT team management capabilities described in Chapter 2. Good team management is an important start but does not reveal the whole picture.

An IT team must also give careful attention to excelling throughout the IT lifecycle, namely in the phases of planning, project delivery, and operations/security.

Next comes the issue of IT to business alignment. As discussed earlier in this chapter, good governance and good relationships are the two vital components of close alignment between IT and the business. Good results without good relationships, and good relationships without good results is just not good enough. And surveys repeatedly show that IT to business alignment is at the top of the CIO's list of priorities.

Finally, there is the aspect of culture in two critical areas, namely continuous service improvement and leadership. These two components are similar but different. Continuous service improvement (and innovation) is primarily about putting new ideas and processes in place to deliver value for the business. IT leadership provides a driving force for effective strategy, projects, and operations, providing inspiration, motivation, and environment for the IT team to deliver their best.

The following list is taken from our "Effective IT Questionnaire." The quotient for measuring continuous service improvement and innovation is extracted from responses in the other areas. You may want to work through this list and highlight which areas you believe are in good shape and which need improvement. (Hint; if you say everything is in good shape, you cannot give yourself high marks for continual service improvement!)

Governance

- Governance processes need to be efficient and appropriate

- Capital and operational budgets are fairly allocated to the highest priorities

- The structure is efficient, with authority at the correct levels

- Governance is supported by the IT leadership team

Business Relationship Management

- The working relationship with business counterparts needs to be good with good cooperation from senior business leaders

- The IT organization needs to be perceived as politics free

- The user help desk has a very good reputation for solving problems, being responsive, and helpful. The customer satisfaction results are good (>75 percent)

- Regular meetings with business counterparts to identify new opportunities in an interactive innovation forum

Project Deliver Excellence

- Projects are delivered close to the original projected completion dates, follow a proven project methodology, and allow for some amendments to the original requirements

- Projects are carefully selected to deliver the best business benefits

- Project managers have authority to deliver projects successfully with proactive and positive governance to remove project blocks

- The IT leadership team works with other managers to lead change

Operational Excellence

- Our IT processes are very well documented and provide a good balance of structure and flexibility

- We look to improve our efficiency to maintain our benchmarked performance in the top quartile

- Our IT systems are very reliable with resilience for key systems and few priority one outages

- Our operational systems gives us good reporting information

Strategy and Planning

- There is a structured process for developing strategy, which is updated and communicated on a regular basis

- Our strategy looks at different options to find the best way forward to improve performance

- We have aggressive stretch targets to improve our KPIs year after year with a line of sight to corporate objectives and priorities. We are regularly updated on what the company is doing and its plans

- Our vision is clear and well communicates what it means for us in practice

Maximizing Potential

- Our people are always in the right posts

- We actively promote people to maximize their potential and have succession plans in place

- We have a formal scheme for mentoring and coaching for everyone in the IT department

- We have very good technical understanding, expertise, and knowledge Team Spirit

- Our IT leadership team is highly visible to the IT staff members and fully supported by them

- Staff enjoy their work. There is a good team spirit and mutual trust, and the IT team often meets outside of work

- We share knowledge freely, record lessons learned, and learn from each other

- We have a good relationship with our vendors and listen to their problems

Team Management Essentials

- We sometimes recruit under qualified staff because our pay scales are not competitive. We often have recruitment vacancies that take significant time and effort to fulfill

- Our recruitment process has been developed in collaboration with HR and provides a range of tests for candidates that have proven effective

- We have a good IT organizational structure that meets the needs of the business

- There is a code of conduct/behavior for IT staff members, and our managers actively manage performance and provide positive feedback

6.3 *EXCELLENT IT MANAGEMENT* - LEADERSHIP OPPORTUNITIES

IT leaders have developed the concept of the "leadership opportunity," a type of activity that sets a leader apart from everyone else. Leadership opportunities appear in all aspects of our work, and successful leaders spend a significant amount of their time on them. Leadership opportunities come to everyone, but not everyone recognizes them for what they are. Only those who are smart will take advantage of them. And if you really want to get ahead, you will need to create your own.

In our skills model, we have identified ten roles that successful IT managers play in different amounts. Five were described in our first book, *Excellent IT Management*, and five as part of this one, *Excellent IT Leadership*.

The first set of suggestions are leadership opportunities from the five roles described in *Excellent IT Management*. The list has been created and developed by delegates over the last five years.

6.3.1 IT Strategist

Strategy is considered to be the most important leadership skill of a chief executive. It should also be one of your priorities.

Understand and Verify the Plan: The first step in reviewing the plan is to ensure that you have a copy of the most recent business strategy. Familiarize yourself with what it says, and keep a one-page summary close at hand. Look at both the top-level business strategy and the functional IT strategy.

Strategic Alignment: Compare the business-level strategy with the IT strategy, and identify the points of alignment. Identify two or three actions to improve alignment.

Culture: One of the most neglected areas of strategy formulation is that of culture. Where it exists, identify statements of culture from the strategy document, and look for ways to embed this within the organization.

Developing Strategy: Developing a strategy for your own area of responsibility is a massive opportunity, providing the opportunity to work with your team and key sponsors around the business. Always look for ways to improve the plan by asking the question, "Is there a better way?"

Communicating Strategy: To use an analogy, creating strategy without communicating it is like building a bicycle without a seat. It is important that everyone who needs to be informed is fully apprised of the business and IT strategy. If possible, take the opportunity to work with the other senior business leaders to present strategy to the organization at large. Use the plot on a page and similar techniques to ensure that your strategy outputs are clear and memorable.

6.3.2 Project and Business Change Leader

Inspire Change: In order to foster a culture of change, it is important to create a strong desire to change, helping everyone to understand why the standards of today are not sufficient to achieve success in the future. Take time to review your leading competitors, not just the largest but also the most innovative. Identify reasons why they will continue to grow their market share, and use this as a catalyst to drive change.

Speak to the Users: As often as you can, take the opportunity to spend time with the employees who actually use the systems. If possible, work on the front line with them for a day. This may include answering phone calls from customers or going out with field engineers to resolve problems. This will not only give you a clear insight into the problems that the users encounter but will also boost your credibility and profile around the organization.

Review the Existing Programs: Review the leadership and change programs currently within your organization and compare how each of them is faring against the checklist of business change success. The reality is that most business change programs fail for the same reasons. It is the job of the technology leader to act as a font of knowledge for what makes a change program successful. Implement a project portfolio management system to keep a close handle on the priority projects.

Benefits Realization: It is vital that all change programs deliver against the benefits on which they were approved. This requires a regular review of all programs. Programs should be assessed on a clear, fair, and repeatable basis. Meetings need to be scheduled regularly so that a culture of continuous improvement is developed. Lessons learned should be properly documented and available for all program managers and business change leaders in the future.

Office of the Future: Set up a space, or create an animation to show what the office of the future will look like.

6.3.3 Performance Pioneer

Survey Your Users: As an IT manager, you will want to provide good service and value for money for your users. Canvass regular feedback from the users. Speak to them on a one-to-one basis, asking questions about what they like about IT and what annoys them. Consider running a survey and questionnaire at least once a year. Carefully phrase the questions, and be smart in how you interpret the responses. For example, one company lists the top five issues that came out of the survey the previous year and asks if the respondent feels that these are still the top five, and if not, which ones have changed.

Measure Your Process Efficiency: Think about where IT spends its time and money. Break down the work of the whole department into sub-processes, and calculate how long each process takes on average, how many resources it consumes, and how much it costs as a result. Use this to identify opportunities for process improvement. Work with the rest of your team to implement the best ideas. Extend this analysis to the rest of the business. Remember that IT is in a unique situation in that it sees how all the processes across the organization operate. Chances are that many of the more expensive processes are aligned to less profitable parts of the business. If this is the case, look to develop ideas to resolve this.

Root Cause Analysis: Identify your top five incident types, and identify the top five root causes. Set up a plan to either fix them completely or reduce them significantly. You may want to look at business process engineering techniques as a way of achieving this.

Review Systems: Think about the results that your team is measured on. Verify that these are accurately aligned to the priorities of the business. For example, one of our clients, a CIO who had just started a new job at a large insurance company, found that technical staff was rewarded on the number of incidents they resolved. He changed the performance paradigm to measure people against how many incidents they prevented from happening in the first place.

Ride with the Engineer: In the telecom industry, managers are encouraged to "ride with the engineer," in other words, take a day out to see how the business really operates at the front line. Other businesses also do this, such as hotel chains and retail companies. It can provide a unique insight into the effectiveness of the company in its processes and how it carries them out for customers, as well as building relationships across the company. One company provided expertise from the IT department to help one of its clients implement a document management system that had already been successful in its own organization. You can take this to an extreme with an exchange program, swapping members of your team with other departments or other companies.

6.3.4 Crisis Commander

Create a Crisis Communication Pack: As part of a campaign to improve customer awareness of how to respond in a crisis, create a crisis communication pack containing key contact names, crisis support process, etc. A number of companies have compressed this into a document that folds to the size of a credit card, so it can be kept in an employee's wallet.

Review the Existing Contingency Plans: Successful crisis leadership depends on good planning. Good plans are not necessarily detailed plans. It is important that the plans are practical, accessible, and fully understood by all those who are part of the crisis management process.

Improve Incident Response: If you can avoid crises happening in the first place, you'll be doing yourself a big favor. Many organizations continue to resolve the same issues, wasting time, money, and other resources. Look back over the last twenty-four months of operation, and list the major outages that have been encountered. With the senior incident and crisis management team, review how these happened, and verify that the root cause analysis was done and the improvements put in place. If this did not happen, take steps to rectify the situation. Build a "lessons learned" database from these experiences, and share it with the rest of the team.

Role-Play/Simulate Crises: Create different scenarios, and practice them using realistic simulations. There are two very important aspects to handling crises effectively. The first aspect relates to the resolution team, ensuring that they all have the necessary tools, training, facilities, and authorities to fix problems quickly. The second role, which relates more to the crisis leader, is that of communication. There is no substitute for practice. The more lifelike the simulation, the more valuable the training experience. Participants need to gain experience in resolving the large number of issues present in any serious crisis situation under extreme time pressure.

6.3.5 Commercial Expert

Train Together: Of the leaders who attend our leadership program, less than 30 percent have never attended formal negotiation training. Although most organizations have a professional procurement department to carry out many of the sourcing activities, the reality is that many IT managers spend a significant amount of their time negotiating technology contracts. Teams that practice together perform better than those that don't. And teams that negotiate badly can be very expensive.

Create a Common Database of Contracts: Every IT manager needs to have a strong and accurate grasp of all budget lines in his or her responsibility. Typically, 30 to 50 percent of most IT budgets relate to supply contracts. There are many aspects to technology contract management, including contract terms, pricing, and support levels. If you do not have a contracts database already, consider setting one up.

Benchmark Your Organization: Good managers are always on the lookout to do things better. Benchmarking will identify such opportunities. In general, some areas will perform better than the industry and others below the industry average. Regular benchmarking will help to foster a culture of continuous improvement. Audits can provide similar feedback. Always be looking to measure performance, either good or bad. One organization ran a "hack-a-thon" day. The idea was not to breach the security of the company (although this might be another fun activity) but to create an innovative piece of code for the company to use (in this case, sell, as it was a software development company).

Review Current Sourcing Arrangements: Some companies have all their IT services in house, and some are fully outsourced. The majority, however, are right-sourced—in other words, a measured combination of in-house and outsourced services. The point where the balance is struck will depend on many factors, such as the sensitivity of the service, cost-effectiveness, and changing market conditions. Take the opportunity to review current sourcing arrangements every year. It is important for every IT manager to have good facts and data on why current sourcing arrangements exist.

6.4 *EXCELLENT IT LEADERSHIP*—LEADERSHIP OPPORTUNITIES

The following lists leadership opportunities from the five skills described in this book.

6.4.1 Personal Coach

Personal Strengths and Weaknesses: The work of Daniel Goleman on emotional intelligence identifies that managers who understand their strengths and weaknesses are more effective. It is important that you understand yours. This can be done through a 360-degree survey, psychometric tests, or discussions with your manager as part of the review process.

IT Managers Network: Often, the first step for an IT manager to develop his or her personal presence within the IT marketplace is to become part or all of a professional group. Examples can include IT directors' forums and industry and professional associations. Other options include LinkedIn. LinkedIn is a massive business network and also includes an IT leaders forum for former delegates to share information.

Industry Profile: Successful IT professionals often have a high profile outside of their own organization. Look for opportunities to raise your

profile at industry conferences, seminars, and other events. Build yourself a reputation in an area of expertise that interests you, such as a particular technology or innovation.

Write a Paper: Think about writing a technical paper, either for publication in a main IT journal or for distribution in your company (or both). You may wish to ask your PR department if they can advise which publications may be interested in this. If they are companies that you buy advertising in, this will make publication somewhat easier.

Charity Work: Many CIOs also do charity work; examples include the *Computer Weekly* overnight event in the UK in support of the homeless and recycling old computers for third world educational markets.

Network of Suppliers: It is vital for every IT manager to build his or her network of contacts outside the peer group of IT managers. Examples of a good network of contacts include technology suppliers, senior headhunters, and directors of other organizations. Take every opportunity to join senior-level briefings from your major technology providers. Get to know the major recruitment firms of IT managers—there are about ten firms responsible for recruiting the most senior posts. A number of them offer breakfast meetings where you get the chance to meet other IT director peers. A list of these major recruitment firms is given on the IT Leaders website, http://www.itleaders.co.uk.

Sources of Learning: Senior IT managers have a thirst for knowledge and a strong motivation to keep improving the way things are. Think about your own sources of learning. These should include business journals as well as IT publications. The *Financial Times*, *The New York Times*, and *The Economist* provide high-quality sources of both business and technical developments. The technical press, such as *CIO* magazine, *Computer Weekly*, and *Computing* provide more in-depth information on the world of IT. A number of CIOs also look to technical reference sites and Internet blogs for further information. Management and leadership courses, particularly if focused for information technology professionals, provide a great opportunity for skills development. Think also about how to build your knowledge of your company. Put the quarterly financial results reporting dates in your calendar, and take time to study new financial reports when they are issued. You should always have the up-to-date facts and figures about your organization in your head.

6.4.2 Technology Innovator

As a senior manager in the world of technology, people will often look to you as a source of technical knowledge for today and technology innovation for the future.

Time for Innovation: Reserve time in your schedule to think about different possibilities. Keep asking the question, Is there a better way of doing this? Use the scenario-planning techniques. For example, looking at the problem the other way, how could we improve efficiency by 30 percent, or reduce costs by 30 percent, or increase sales by 30 percent? Google are reported as allowing all their staff time completely free of their work obligations each month to work on new ideas to benefit the business. This scheme has been responsible for generating some of the most successful ideas for the company.

Keep Abreast of New Technology and Innovation: Think about the technologies you believe will be the strongest influences within your organization. Meet with leading technology providers, together with your team, to identify the opportunities that new developments and innovations in technology can bring.

Spread the Word: Encourage your team members to speak to the rest of the business about the possibilities that technology can offer today and in the future. Encourage them to meet with managers on a semi-regular basis to talk about such issues

Create a Sense of Urgency: Identify something that you believe you should be looking into and create the sense of urgency that might spur your organization into action.

Technology Road Show: One of the CIOs of a leading insurance company put a technology road show in place for his company. He asked everyone in his team to identify a new technology that might benefit the company in some way. When they were ready, they invited the rest of the company to look at what was possible. The result was a significant increase in credibility and dialogue with the business. Another idea is to create videos showcasing new technologies.

Innovation Workshop: Once or twice a year, invite a small group of influential managers from all departments to brainstorm new possibilities. Approach it from both angles. Look out for business opportunities that need a technology solution as well as technology opportunities that can be applied to solve business problems. Keep the discussion focused on resolving specific problems. Additionally, you could be instrumental in setting up an electronic suggestions scheme. Review all ideas regularly, and put incentives in place to encourage new ideas. One company has a regular Friday afternoon innovation workshop get together for the whole company. Another used an investment review panel to encourage employees and partners to present new ideas that might be valuable for the company.

White Papers: If there is a particular technology that either is about to be or should be adopted by your organization, take the initiative and write a white paper to explain how it works and the benefits it would bring. Publish it in the company newsletter, if appropriate. Similarly, consider offering to write or publish case studies from your organization in respected journals of IT management or present it at a conference.

Create Something Innovative: One organization developed a small smart phone application that allowed senior managers to update and manage a key process in the organization in real time. Another created an animation showing what their organization might look like in the future. One hotel chain created an animation of a hotel of the future to illustrate how technology would influence their business.

6.4.3 Team Captain

There are many possible leadership opportunities in the area of team leadership. Here are some ideas to get you started.

Change the Environment: The environment your team works in plays an important role in their productivity. It is easy to think that the environment cannot be changed. It is usually true that office leases mean that it is not possible to move location. However, there are many things you can do to improve conditions within the building. This may require some investment. For example, new furniture, carpets, or pictures, but you may also be able to improve conditions through simple maintenance activities that reduce clutter and noise levels. Some companies have set up special chill-out rooms, and others have crèches with a picture-in-picture cam for parents to monitor their children.

Monitor Performance: Take a step back, and assess the performance of your team. Think about how closely individual objectives are aligned to departmental and company objectives. Check that all team members have the right skills and are properly rewarded for good performance. Perhaps you have a particular member of staff who is experiencing performance problems. Work with them to resolve the problem. It may require training, a change of responsibilities, or more accurate objectives. In all cases, as their manager, you have the right and authority to make this happen.

Induction and Training: Think about how new employees are looked after when they join the company. Do they have a manager and/or mentor assigned to show them how things work. Are they enrolled into the key company inductions programs? Is there an induction program for IT that explains the department's strategy and the key business processes, such as ITIL or PRINCE II? One opportunity is to create a workshop on what company values mean and how they work in practice.

Coaching: You will have many opportunities for coaching your staff. These may include team meetings or interdepartmental meetings. Fully brief your direct reports, and identify two or three coaching points that

they should focus on when the meeting takes place. Your coaching style will depend on the team member. Less-experienced staff will need more specific instructions; experienced team members should be guiding the discussion and identifying their own points of priority.

Motivation: As the team manager, you are responsible for the motivational levels of your staff. This can take many forms—team dinners, for example, or an offsite seminar or conference. Ensure that these are properly planned. It is easy for motivational sessions to become counter-productive because of poor planning. One IT team organized a "treasure hunt" around London (using a similar idea to the film *National Treasure* starring Nicholas Cage, where clues were arranged at different locations) for the company, providing an excellent opportunity to meet peers across the organization.

Team Meetings: Team meetings offer an excellent opportunity for building rapport. One option is to plan your own workshop—asking someone on your own team to share his or her knowledge with other team members on, say, a new technology or corporate program. Another opportunity for IT team meetings is to host a "technology showcase"—inviting key vendors to ask them about technology futures, roadmaps, and advances that are being implemented in peer (competitor) organizations.

Recognize Great Results: Create a platform to recognize great results, for example, via the intranet, or create a "wall of awesome" board, as one company has.

6.4.4 Executive connector

Business relationship management offers the greatest opportunity for career enhancement.

Create a Network Plan: Use the techniques described in Chapter 4 to identify your existing contacts and highlight new key contacts you need to get to know better. Look for opportunities to build bridges with them, such as helping them to resolve problems or working on common projects.

Plot Your Network: Information passes across organizations according to the book, *The Tipping Point*, through a combination of mavens and connectors. Mavens are the highly intelligent sources of information. Connectors are those people who know a lot of people within an organization, usually a cross departmental and other boundaries. As a technology manager, you will often be considered a technical or informational expert and all the more reason why you should also develop your profile as a connector. Plot your circle of influence. Identify everyone you know there as either high, medium, or low; those marked high are your closest circle, and those marked low represent those people whose name you know but who you only meet from time to time.

Create Campaigns of Influence: Think about difficult decisions that need to be made. Create a campaign of influence to target the key decision makers. Work with your colleagues, so points are put across from different sources, making them more acceptable. If you don't have direct contact with any particular decision makers, identify who of your supporters do and encourage them to help you.

Faire le Point: The French have an expression called *faire le point*, which literally means to make the point. It refers to the short (typically fifteen minutes) but regular meetings that senior managers have with each other. When I worked in France, I was struck by how closely bonded the senior management team was. These regular meetings were at the heart of this. There was not necessarily a specific agenda, just a mutual agreement to share information and talk about new developments and opportunities.

Manage by Opportunity: Be on the lookout for situations that make it easier to get difficult things done. For example, if the company finds it difficult to invest in backup hardware, use system downtime to emphasize the risks to the business of not having a backup plan in place.

Identify Targets: Identify two or three managers within your organization who are highly influential. They should be people you don't know particularly well. Look for opportunities to build bridges with them, helping them to resolve particular problems or working on common projects.

Create an Easy-to-Use IT Manual: Create a manual for users, explaining key aspects of the IT processes, what to do in a crisis, and key aspects of the in-house systems. Posters can also be a useful communications channel to inform users how to best contact the IT department.

Keep Up to Date: It is important to keep up to date with the priorities of every department and to take every opportunity to build relationships with other heads of department. One option is to invite the other heads of department to your regular management meetings. Organize this properly, so they aren't sitting through a long discussion on data center operations.

Business Travel: If you are travelling on business, identify if any other work colleagues or peers are also at the same location, and take the opportunity to go meet up with them out of hours.

How Did We Do?: Set up discussions for post implementation reviews. Think about how both sides can operate better to deliver better results next time. (This should not be a "beat up IT" session, but an interactive discussion)!

6.4.5 Business Champion

Corporate leadership is a very broad topic, and the involvement of an IT leader will very much depend on the organization. However, at its highest level, it is about governing guiding and shaping the business.

Get Involved in Board Issues: Many CIOs get hung up with being a member of the board. The reality is that they will be invited when they have a contribution to make. Board meetings are about securing business success, and therefore, contributions are focused on which areas around the business will have the highest impact. Every senior IT manager will be required to join a board meeting from time to time. It is important to take full advantage of this opportunity. Conversely, presentations need to be short and brief. Contributions need to be insightful and to the point. If the IT executive focuses on the business priorities, the likelihood is they will continue to be invited back.

Get Involved in Company-Wide Governance: Identify which review meetings you can delegate to your team and which others you might benefit from, in terms of building your profile at a more senior level.

Think About Strategy: IT executives are in a privileged position of being able to see all of the processes that make up an organization's operation. Use this opportunity to good advantage, reviewing areas where improvements can be made. Pay particular attention to the key metrics that are laid out in the top-level business strategy. Look for opportunities to help attain these objectives, and meet with other senior directors to discuss them.

Look at Corporate Risk: Risk in an organization is often fragmented. Holistic methods of corporate risk management, such as ABCD analysis, should be considered. These allow the most important risks affecting the business to be identified and mitigated. Review how your organization currently handles risk, and assess the value of implementing such an integrated risk management approach.

Think About Portfolio Management: IT managers are usually involved in most projects. But as the priorities of an organization change, the value of these projects will go up and down. It is important that projects are reviewed and prioritized on a regular basis to ensure that the resources of the business are targeted in the best way possible. Remember, one of the most difficult leadership decisions you can make is to stop a project. But we have observed that the more senior and effective the manager, the better they are at making these decisions.

Join in with Out-of-Hours Activities: Being part of the company sports and social club, playing on squash ladders, and so on, can offer opportunities for getting to know people outside of your immediate circle of influence. Many of the CIOs we interviewed were heavily involved in the company's nominated charities, and some of them have set up company charities for IT-related assistance, such as offering old refurbished PCs to charities and providing PC training for young people in the neighborhood to help them with job opportunities.

How Compliant Are You?: Compliance is a complex and difficult puzzle. What are the main compliance requirements of your business? Summarize what needs to be done in all areas. Some compliance, for example, data protection and security are almost exclusively the responsibility of IT. It can be helpful to set a baseline for compliance, so that compliance in one year means compliance in subsequent years, unless audit or senior management has an approval for a new standard. Look to bring together all the compliance requirements in one place, and set up a compliance group to monitor activities against the objectives.

Corporate Social Responsibility: Create a campaign demonstrating how IT can support or lead CSR activities.

Communicate Your Achievements: IT managers are often so busy delivering projects and keeping systems operational that they forget to keep the business informed of success. Although one doesn't wish to be immodest, it is still important to keep everyone informed of the improvements that have taken place. You would be surprised how little senior executives are aware of IT's achievements, unless they are specifically told. Work with the business to advertise your joint project successes. One IT group installed plasma screens around the offices, including reception, that could promote the company's successes, including IT initiatives.

Escalation Management: Make senior management aware of important issues. This may require you to escalate things through your organization. Be careful how you do this, as you will be transcending different management layers. However, there is an excellent article in Harvard Business Review on IBM's Web Pioneers, which tells the story of how a small group of IBMers managed to persuade their senior executive to adopt the Internet and online services after *Sun* used their data feed at the Lillehammer Winter Olympics.

Work with Senior Executives: All of the CIOs we interviewed recently stated they were involved in their company's charity initiatives. Some also have their own initiatives, such as providing IT training for local people or contracts for recycling their old PCs for charity. Another IT team collects equipment offered by vendors and raffle them each year for their company's charity.

Help Senior Executives: The plain fact is that the senior board members of any company have the most influence and can be extremely helpful in promoting one's career, and conversely, slowing it down if one does not have a good reputation. Take the opportunity to go the extra mile for the senior executives. Examples from previous groups include installing individual software productivity packages on their laptops, configuring phones for special applications, or installing computer equipment at their homes.

Corporate events: Keep an eye open for the key events that your organization is involved with and seek to join where appropriate. Examples include product launches, financial results postings, conferences, and exhibitions.

6.5 THE FIRST NINETY DAYS

A lot of our work is with new CIOs and IT directors, supporting them in their new roles and providing guidance during the initial, critical time. This critical time is known as the first ninety days (the term, "The first 100 days," is often used on television news stations, particularly when monitoring the progress of a new president.) The guidelines that follow have been built from our work in this area. I hope you find them interesting and valuable. They look at the immediate priorities (the tactics) and the planning activities needed to ensure long-term success.

The first ninety days in a new role as the leader of any team are probably the most critical—get them wrong, and you risk failure. Get them right, and you will enjoy and thrive in your new role. The guidelines were created for a new CIO. Many of the activities will be relevant for all IT management posts, but in some cases, they are CIO-specific, so you may

wish to modify them for different assignments. The sequence and timings are merely a guideline and will change from post to post and company to company.

6.5.1 Why Is This a Critical Time?

Any new role or job, whether within your existing business or joining a new company, presents a unique opportunity to make a positive and lasting impression. A positive impression will give you a flying start toward gaining acceptance of a new strategy and changes to working practices. There is only one chance to make a first impression—get the first few months wrong, and it could impact your relationships with others for a very long time, creating doubters and resisters to change.

During a period of transition, the team you will be joining will probably have few preconceptions. People typically have an open mind and are willing to try new ideas, giving you the benefit of the doubt. We often see this phenomenon when consultants are called in to resolve a critical business issue. They often say exactly the same things as the internal managers, but as outsiders, their views are respected and acted upon.

Your recent appointment to the role may well mean you have less idea of what needs to be done than others who work for you! Your lack of knowledge and expertise makes you vulnerable to getting decisions wrong. On every team there is be a mixture of people and politics. Getting the right people on your side makes driving the strategy through to implementation much easier.

There will be a lot to do in a short period of time, and you may well feel overwhelmed by it all. Many managers suffer from what is called "imposter syndrome," a fictitious affliction that makes them feel they are not up to their new job. Don't worry about it. Be smart, and use the expertise of your previous assignments, and make the best use of your team. Most effective managers rely heavily on their informal networks, but in the early stages of a new job, these don't exist, so work energetically on building them.

Because people often give the benefit of the doubt to those who are starting a new job or joining a new team, things often go well for a period of time. If you make mistakes, they will forgive you because you're new to the job. This is referred to as the "honeymoon period." However, after a period of time (the first ninety days), you will need to perform well, meeting the expectations of key stakeholders. Ninety days is almost no time at all to make the necessary preparations for future success. So, no time to hang around then!

6.5.2 Before You Start

Negotiate the foundation of your success before you start. Be streetwise when negotiating a new employment contract. Get commitments from your new boss on what exactly is expected. Understand why your predecessor didn't succeed (assuming this was the case). If you have been brought in to fix particular problems, get the root of them early, commit to fixing them, and assign the necessary resources.

Do some planning and preparation before your start date. If you are starting work for a new company, take time to properly understand the business. Work through the financial reports of the company (all companies have to file their accounts, even if privately owned), look at the company website, and find out about industry trends.

On the first day, your priority is to confirm your responsibilities and clarify budget and resources with your boss. Look for clarity on what is required and when. From this, you will be able to identify the work priorities and potential problems. Develop a personal to-do list of things to get ready or put in place.

Think also about how you might need to change from the role you did previously—different behaviors you need to exhibit. For example, new technical or industry knowledge or new skills. Understanding these things early will help you succeed early.

Whatever your IT management role, use the following suggestions to put together a plan for your first ten weeks in your new position. The

activities have been divided into different phases. These should be treated merely as a guideline. Some activities may be done in a different order. Think carefully about what needs to be done, and act decisively. This is your opportunity to impress, so don't rush in without preparation. One of my favorite expressions for these situations is, "Do it once, and do it right!"

6.5.3 Weeks One and Two

Meet Your Boss: Spend time with your new boss. Prepare well for these meetings. Understand his or her priorities, and outline what you propose to do in your first weeks. Your boss will be able to set up meetings for you to meet your key business stakeholders. Get some indication of your objectives. If you are replacing someone in the role, find out what worked and what didn't for your predecessor. Now is the time to ask what the key governance meetings are, and join them where appropriate. It is quite possible that your predecessor is still working in the organization (they may even be your boss), and you should take the opportunity to meet with them. Think carefully about what you learn, and make your own considered judgment about what needs to change and what can remain.

Get to Know Your Team: Meet with your direct reports at the earliest opportunity. Use this opportunity to introduce yourself and outline what you hope to achieve in the next few weeks. Ask them if they have any pressing concerns, but don't make this meeting a long one. You will have little knowledge of what needs to be done, so you will be guessing. Your primary output from this meeting should be to meet with them all individually over the next few days.

In these early meetings, focus on their current objectives. Don't let them be distracted by your arrival. Ask them what their current priorities are; I often use the question, "What's on your radar?" It is a slightly vague question, and it can prompt some interesting replies. Find out how they think things might be improved. Use this meeting to identify who is well connected in the rest of the business and who is best placed to join you when you meet the other senior managers and sponsors. Finally, keep an eye out for which managers are performing and which may need some particular attention and support.

Arrange to Meet the Key Players: Many of the managers you need to meet will be booked up for the next couple of weeks, so better to get a place in their schedule as a matter of priority. Be prepared to work long hours and travel in order to get time with these people. Look for opportunities to spend time with them outside the immediate work environment where it makes sense. This can often produce very interesting and useful information. This is also a week to get hold of the background information, to look at business reports, and previous strategy documents, if they exist.

Find the Main Operational Issues and Check the Numbers: Find out the main operational issues that affect IT. Start to gather information on the IT group's performance. Think if you need to do an audit using either the internal audit function of the company if one exists, or bring in experts. Check all your numbers, and check with the users about if what you see on your reports is what they experience. Identify the burning issues, and put a short plan together. Use the opportunity for independent reviews (audit, benchmarks, etc.).

Housekeeping: Your final priority this week, particularly if you are new to the company, is to get the housekeeping issues sorted out. You need a desk, ideally near the senior management team you will be working with. Sort out your technology, including a (laptop) computer and a good-quality phone. Attend any induction programs that the company has in place this week, if possible, or, if not, put yourself down on the list of attendees for the earliest free date. The sooner you learn about the company and its culture, the better. You will then be free to focus on the task at hand in the weeks ahead.

6.5.4 Weeks Three and Four

Meet Your Peers: One of your most important tasks is to meet with the other senior managers in the company to understand their priorities and what they expect from the IT department. Don't meet with other

managers if you are not prepared; you will only look foolish and naive. It will probably require a week or two to identify who your key stakeholders are and get ready for these first meetings. Keep them informal, and arrange to meet them on a regular (typically once a month) basis.

First impressions are really important, so draft an agenda, but keep in mind the need to be flexible. Your preparation of last week should stand you in good stead. Take one of your trusted managers with you for support; successful teams hunt in pairs. This will help you to focus on listening; it is very difficult to pick up the nuances of what is being said when you are writing things down. Your colleague should also be able to pick up on some of the issues that arise in the course of the meeting.

For each of the managers, try to find out how well IT performs for them and how it could be improved. Often, the feedback at this stage is around the "how" things are done, (e.g., not very efficient or friendly) rather than the "what." Don't make too many promises at this stage. Find out if they have any personal issues that will allow you to build your relationship with them.

Key outcomes include the following:

1. Their view of the business at the present time and how they see the business-wide challenges in the near and longer term. Ask them what they think IT can deliver that it doesn't currently.

2. An understanding of their own role in the organization and their targets for the year. "What keeps you awake at night?" is a good question to get a different perspective on their priorities.

3. An insight into how the role has been performed in the past and their views on it, specifically how it can be improved and what you can do to help.

Use this meeting to outline how you propose to develop your plans and get their agreement. Remember, it's very much an outline, so don't fence yourself in by being too specific. You will also need their commitment to attend the necessary meetings and make their people available.

Your final task is to ask them if there is any further information they think is important, and ask if they can suggest others who could assist you. It's always easier to get someone's cooperation when you are introduced to them by a senior manager.

Try to keep the door open (metaphorically) after each meeting. It is too easy when you have several meetings set up with new colleagues to lose the initial momentum. Copy your notes from the meeting within twenty-four hours, and ask for their agreement to what you have noted. If they are key people, phone them regularly to keep them informed about your progress.

Think About Targets: Sometime early on in week two, you should be shaping your thinking on what needs to be done. You may want to convert this into some high-level objectives. Objectives should be personal, IT specific, and business-related. Personal objectives (those done predominantly through your actions) might include improving morale; IT objectives might include improving customer satisfaction, reducing call incident levels; business objectives might business objectives include revenue or growth targets or process improvement. If you are setting your objectives at a personal level, it may be smart to speak to your boss. For IT and business objectives, gather the stakeholders together early on.

Use the discussion about objectives to get to know your own team better. Arrange one-on-one meetings with them to discuss their objectives, which should already be written in their personal development plans. Look to set challenges for those who are up to it. Make a rational assessment of each of your direct reports, so you have good facts and data to act on if you need to reorganize.

Set Up Governance: Spend the first couple of weeks understanding the governance in place. Work out what works and what doesn't, and firm up a regular meeting schedule. Set up regular (IT) reviews, so you

understand what the main project and operational issues are, what your team is spending time on, and the progress being made.

Verify with the business sponsors which projects are the most important. Secondly, identify the most important operational issues in the department, and get the relevant managers to put a plan together to fix them; don't be tempted to try and fix them yourself!

Start Review of Risk, Compliance, and Audit: As part of the governance, you have the ideal opportunity to kick off a number of assignments to find out more formally how things are delivering. Use internal audit to get brownie points and external audits to get industry comparison, and set the benchmark for the future.

6.5.5 Weeks Five and Six

Start Work on Your Plan: You will need to start by gaining an understanding of the business strategy. Review the IT strategy that is hopefully in place. Think about setting up an offsite workshop with your team to put some structure around your strategic planning process. Let all the participants know what they will need to bring to the meeting. Do not make it too onerous for them, but be clear on what preparation is required.

Choose your venue carefully and either visit it beforehand, or get someone else to do it for you; check out the facilities, break out rooms, coffee/lunch break timings, and directions to get there. If you are running the meeting at your office, check the logistics, including equipment, such as projectors and flip charts.

Copy the minutes within twenty-four hours, and contact each of the members to get their feedback and recommitment to deliver on what they agreed to do.

Keep Contact with Senior Business Sponsors: Keep them updated of your plans. It needn't take too long, a fifteen-minute coffee or lunch, but keep up the communication. It is all too easy to let these key contacts drift off because you are so busy with other things. If possible, arrange to meet them at least once a month—faire le point, as the French say, and do! Your strategy work should be developing, and you should be able to play back some of your ideas as to how the business objectives might be met.

Review the Organizational Structure: You may need to make some changes to how your team is organized. Take the necessary time to do this correctly, or you may make the wrong decision. Some managers may appear unsettled or nervous, so take time with them to understand their concerns. Try to inspire them and give them confidence. However, if after six weeks, they are still very dependent on you ("time-consuming managers"), see if there is a better way to use their talents in a different role. Some managers may appear awkward or hostile. Don't spend much time appeasing them. Find them another job in another department, or help them to exit the company. Some IT senior managers ask for the right to bring in their own management team (usually only one or two) in order to spread a new way of working to the IT team.

It is important to recognize, that at more senior levels in an organization, managers can fail in their function due to their style and fit in the organization, and it is no reflection on their individual talents. Although initially it may seem unfair, it is often better for them to find new opportunities elsewhere than continue in a role they are not suited to. The work in weeks five and six may be around identifying options and verifying the capabilities of your direct reports. Put together your "dream team" on paper. Identify where you have major skill gaps and need to recruit.

Make Some Decisions About Rogue Projects: In most organizations, there are a number of projects that started with good intentions but for any number of reasons are not delivering the expected benefits. The reasons for this can be various—not enough resources, poor project management, poorly defined requirements, suspect business case, or very often, a change in business conditions, meaning the project priority has fallen off. We find that the more experienced a manager, the more likely he is to cancel these projects. Have a review with the key sponsors (or do it one on one) to reduce your current portfolio. This will also free up space that you will probably need as your IT strategy develops.

6.5.6 Weeks Seven and Eight

Develop the First Cut of the Strategic Plan: Your workshop from earlier should have given a good baseline from which to develop the strategy. You should be receiving back the near-final proposals from each of your first line reports that you should look to consolidate. Look for conflicts, and normalize the resource.

In Weeks Seven and Eight, You Should Be Able to Do the Following:

1. Confirm the business and IT objectives you will deliver against

2. Have a full list of current projects and their priorities

3. Identify a list of potential projects required to deliver the objectives

4. Put together a provisional (first cut) budget and resourcing plan Look at reducing risk and doing it better.

Get Approval for the New Organization: Make time to meet with the head of HR to review your thoughts on the current organization. Ask for the view of the HR director. Verify if your provisional organization is the right one. Get agreement to hire in new managers where required.

6.5.7 Weeks Nine to Twelve

Finalize the Strategic Plan: Verify enough activities against all of the individual objectives. Meet with each of the stakeholders to inform them of what you are doing for them.

Review Risk, Compliance, and Audit Work: The risk process that was initiated in the meeting of week four should now be formalized. Create a risk register of the top risks (up to a maximum of twenty), and if too many risks are identified, the task becomes too cumbersome and usually ends up on the "too difficult" pile. Many successful teams only manage their top ten risks.

Look to integrate any key findings into your IT strategy.

Sign-Off the IT Strategy: In week ten, look to get sign-off for your plan. This is a highly critical stage. Don't ask for a blank signature without explaining the consequences.

You should look for agreement of the following:

1. Sign-off of the high-level objectives

2. Agreement of the key initiatives, how they align, and the joint project plan

3. Validation of the risk register with key risks

4. Approval for the necessary resources and budget

5. Commitment from senior execs for their involvement and support in the governance process

7. In Conclusion

7.1 TAKE TIME TO REFLECT

THIS BOOK CAN ONLY PROVIDE A SUMMARY OF IT MANAGEMENT AND OFFERS PROVEN GUIDELINES THAT WE HAVE FOUND WORK well. Depending on your current role, company, or situation, some ideas will be more relevant than others. Look to develop your own thinking in this area, adapted to your own style and organization.

7.2 NEXT STEPS

Hopefully, you have identified some ideas you can put into practice. Think carefully about your own career development and that of your team. Consider what would have the most significant benefit and be easy to implement. Then make a simple to-do list with timings for completion.

7.3 AND FINALLY

If you found this book valuable or would like some advice on any of the topics, please feel free to e-mail me at david.mckean@itleaders.co.uk.

Good luck!
David McKean

8. Bibliography

FOLLOWING ARE SOME RECOMMENDED BOOKS AND PAPERS THAT HAVE BEEN SOURCES OF KNOWLEDGE AND INSPIRATION.

Personal Coach

Daniel Goleman, "What Makes a Leader?," *Harvard Business Review*, 1998. A ground-breaking assessment of the five key general leadership skills that deliver outstanding results and make the difference

Tom Rath. *Strengths Finder 2.0.* Washington, DC: Gallup Press, 2007. Tom Rath discusses the key management strengths required for business success. The book comes with an electronic code, so you can do an online assessment of your own strengths and weaknesses. By understanding what you excel at and what gives you energy is vital to fulfilling your potential.

Robert Kriegel and Marilyn Kriegel, *The Competition Zone: Peak Performance Under Pressure*. Ballantine Books, 1994. An interesting look at the winning characteristics of high-performing athletes, and in particular, their ability to stay in the Competition ("C") zone, avoiding repetition (drone zone) and panic.

Steven R. Covey, *The 7 Habits of Highly Effective People.* RosettaBooks, 2009. A pioneering book on what makes a successful manager. Stephen Covey invented the principle of quadrant two activities, important but not yet urgent activities, which sets effective managers apart.

IT Leaders. *Leadership Time: the Story of Leo & Michael*. DVD, IT Leaders, 2009.
Available through the IT Leaders website, this video illustrates the IT leadership behaviors of successful CIOs by contrasting the actions of two managers working in parallel companies.

Sue Knight. *NLP at Work, the Essence of Excellence*. Nicholas Brealey Publishing, 2009.
Sue Knight is a leading thinker and author in the world of neurolinguistic programming, the management science of reprogramming our minds to deliver outstanding results.

Team Captain

Malcolm Gladwell, *Blink*. Penguin, 2006.
When we leap to a decision or have a hunch, our unconscious is sifting through the situation in front of us, looking for a pattern, throwing out the irrelevant information, and zeroing in on what really matters. Malcolm Gladwell has a compelling and readable style. *Blink* is filled with fascinating stories, where gut instinct can find answers that logical processes cannot.

SFIA. *Skills Framework for the Information Age*, SFIA, 2010.
More information on SFIA can be found on their website, www.sfia.org.uk. SFIA is the intellectual property of the SFIA Foundation, a not-for-profit organization that distributes SFIA free of charge to end users.

Charles J. Pellerin. *How NASA Builds Teams*. Wiley, 2009.
Charles Pellerin looks at some of the causes of leadership failure, including the problems of the Hubble spacecraft project he headed. He also puts forward a model of leadership profiles, illustrating the fact that if we understand the leadership profile of others, we can increase our influence.

Malcolm Gladwell, *Outliers: the Story of Success*. Penguin, 2009.
Another fascinating and highly readable book from Malcolm Gladwell that discusses the factors that have made people successful. It challenges

the belief that success is purely related to individual talent but more the product of a series of fortuitous events.

Patrick Lencioni, *The Five Dysfunctions of a Team.* Jossey Bass, 2011.
Lencioni offers explicit instructions for overcoming the human behavioral tendencies that corrupt teams.

Meredith Belbin, *Team Roles at Work.* Routledge, 2012.
Belbin's model for understanding the nine roles of successful teams is effective and straightforward. Additional team assessments can be done using the Belbin website, www.belbin.com. This allows individual team members to describe their team skills and preferences. The website then compiles these responses to provide an overall team evaluation, identifying team strengths and potential shortfalls.

Kaplan and Norton, *The Balanced Scorecard, Translating Strategy into Action.* Harvard Business Review Press, 1996.
One of the most famous and important business books of our time. The balanced scorecard promotes leadership thinking by ensuring that organizations focus on long-term results around customers, process excellence, and people, as well as the hard numbers of finance.

Hersey, Blanchard, and Johnson, *Management of Organizational Behavior*, 1996.
Looks in particular at situational leadership, the idea that different team members need different management approaches.

Hargrove, *Masterful Coaching*, 2008.
An interesting book describing coaching techniques using modern thinking.

Jim Collins, *Good to Great*, 2001.
One of my favorite books of all time. Jim Collins carefully selected the best performing (US) companies and identified the critical success factors that put them there.

Executive Connector
Malcolm Gladwell, *The Tipping Point*, 2001.
A compelling book by Malcolm Gladwell that looks at day-to-day problems and identifies that many of them behave like epidemics. They aren't linear phenomena in the sense that they steadily and predictably change. Little things can cause them to "tip" at any time, and if we want to understand how to confront and solve them, we have to understand what those factors are.

Neil Rackham, *Spin Selling*, Gower Publishing, *1995*.
This is a classic sales textbook, but the SPIN technique is an immensely powerful technique for influencing meetings.

Richard Mullender, *Communication Secrets of a Hostage Negotiator*, Griffin Professional Business & Training Services, 2012.
Richard is a fantastic presenter, and his book (properly titled *Dispelling the Myths and Rediscovering the Lost Art of Listening*) will help you do just that. If I was asked to identify *the* most important management skill, it would be the lost art of listening.

Technology Innovator
Peter Drucker, "The Discipline of Innovation," *Harvard Business Review*, August 2002.
A classic paper on the subject of innovation.

Chris Barez-Brown, *How to Have Kick-Ass Ideas*, Skyhorse Publishing, 2008.
An entertaining and creative look at innovation, illustrated with some great case studies.

Roger von Oech, *Creative Whack Pack*, US Games, 1992.
A set of creative ideas on cards. A great way to encourage different ways of thinking to generate new perspectives for solving problems.

Michael Hammer and James Champy. *Reengineering the Corporation*. Nicholas Brealey Publishing, 2001.

A classic book, updated to account for the digital age, recognizing that the new online processes of today are as important as the back office processes of yesterday. Reengineering is a vital concept to understand for IT leaders of today.

Tony Buzan, *The Mind Map Book: Unlock Your Creativity, Boost Your Memory, Change Your Life*, BBC Active, 2009.
All Tony Buzan's books are fascinating, often looking at the characters and attributes of genius. *The Mind Map Book* describes the techniques of mind mapping in a compelling and readable way. Tony Buzan has pioneered mind mapping to draw out concepts that match the natural patterns of our thinking.

Business Champion

"Six IT Decisions Your IT People Shouldn't Make." Jeanne Ross and Peter Weill. *Harvard Business Review*, November, 2002.
A very interesting account to encourage senior business executives to take a serious interest in the key determinants of their technology strategy.

Richard Nolan and Warren McFarlan, "Information Technology and the Board of Directors," *Harvard Business Review*, October 2005.
A look at different governance models, principally determined by an organizations need for high reliability and resilience on the one hand and market agility on the other.

Peter Weill, Jeanne W. Ross, "Strategy, IT Governance and Performance," *Harvard Business Press*, ISBN-13:978-1-8092-1.
An interesting and well-researched look at IT governance with detailed case studies from the financial services industry in particular.

Peter Weill, Jeanne W. Ross, *IT Governance: How Top Performers Manage IT Decision Rights for Superior Results*, Harvard Business Review Press, 2004.

Corporate Governance of Information Technology, ISO/IEC 38500:2008, originally prepared by Standards Australia *(as AS8015:2005)*.
The international standard for IT governance. This high-level document identifies the key principles of successful IT governance. A clear and matter-of-fact description. Exactly what you would expect.

Nassim Nicholas Taleb. *The Black Swan: The Impact of the Highly Improbable.* Penguin, 2008.
An interesting look at events that were considered highly improbable, right up until they happened.

9. About the Author

DAVID MCKEAN IS A FORMER CIO WHO HAS WORKED FOR SEVERAL MUL-
TINATIONAL COMPANIES AROUND THE WORLD, INCLUDING AT&T
Ventures in Asia; UPC Nederland in Holland; and C&W UK. He is now the
managing director of IT Leaders Ltd., a leading provider of IT management
training programs.

In 1994, David joined Cable & Wireless as the program director for the
third GSM license in France, securing one of the most profitable license
wins for Cable & Wireless. Since that time, he has worked for several
international blue-chip companies in Russia, France, Asia, and Holland,
running large strategy development and business change programs. In
Indonesia, in particular, he worked closely with all parts of the culturally
diverse organization to build a business strategy that would meet the
business priorities of all the different stakeholders. It was this work that
led him to recognize the real difficulties that companies have in understanding a clear process for strategy; providing a rigorous and smart strategy; and then having to communicate it to different communities.

David is a regular conference presenter in Europe and Asia on strategy and technology leadership. He is a chartered engineer and a graduate of the University of Cambridge.

David McKean

IT Leaders, Greenlands, Henley-on-Thames, Oxfordshire, RG9 3AU, UK
E-mail: david.mckean@itleaders.co.uk
Telephone: (+44) 1491-57-86-88 (UK) or (+1) 203-810-6143 (US)

Made in the USA
Charleston, SC
22 August 2014